THE TRIUMPH
OF LOVE

John MacArthur
PUBLISHING GROUP
ESTBLD MMXXIII
Los Angeles
CALIFORNIA

DESIGNED BY WEKREATIVE CO.
ISBN: 978-1-883973-08-7
PRINTED IN CHINA

THE TRIUMPH OF LOVE

THE BELIEVER'S VICTORY OVER DOUBT

JOHN MACARTHUR

CONTENTS

INTRODUCTION

All Scripture is God-breathed and spiritually profitable for the salvation and sanctification of every believer. Every word of God is pure truth, living and life-giving, powerful and empowering.

For over half a century, I have lived daily with the Scripture in my hands and on my mind—and preached it from the pulpit of the church—and written a series of expository commentaries on each New Testament book, totaling thirty-four volumes.

I am grateful for everyone who is willing to settle in and dig deep in reading a commentary. But only a few take on such an extensive journey, even though every aspect of the Scripture is life transforming. My desire, however, is for many to engage in such a pursuit because they will then experience the benefit and blessing of the deep dive into a biblical book.

I am certain when people have a taste of the riches of Bible exposition they will want more. So I thought we should give them less to develop the hunger for more.

What do I mean by less?

ONE CHAPTER. ONE MONUMENTAL CHAPTER.

So, that led to the development of this series, *The Great Chapters of the Bible.* This series focuses on key portions of Scripture that establish the foundational truths of the Christian faith. The current volume, adapted from *Romans 1–8*, the MacArthur New Testament Commentary, demonstrates that there is nothing that shall ever "separate us from the love of God, which is in Christ Jesus our Lord" (Rom 8:39).

I believe that exposition of the great chapters of the Bible will lead many to desire to know the rest of each book and to experience the blessing of knowing the Scripture in its fullness.

01

LIFE IN THE SPIRIT—PART 1 THE SPIRIT FREES US FROM SIN AND DEATH AND ENABLES US TO FULFILL THE LAW

ROMANS 8:1–4

There is therefore now no condemnation for those who are in Christ Jesus. For the law of the Spirit of life in Christ Jesus has set you free from the law of sin and of death. For what the Law could not do, weak as it was through the flesh, God did: sending His own Son in the likeness of sinful flesh and as an offering for sin, He condemned sin in the flesh, in order that the requirement of the Law might be fulfilled in us, who do not walk according to the flesh, but according to the Spirit. (8:1–4)

Although the Bible is a book offering the good news of salvation from sin, it is also a book that presents the bad news of condemnation for sin. No single book or collection of writings on earth proclaims so completely and vividly the totally desperate situation of man apart from God.

The Bible reveals that, since the Fall, every human being has been born into the world with a sin nature. What David said of himself can be said of everyone: "Surely I have been a sinner from birth, sinful from the time my mother conceived me" (Ps 51:5 NIV). Earlier in his letter to the Romans, Paul declared, "All have sinned and fall short of the glory of God" (Rom 3:23). Because of that universal and innate sinfulness, all unbelievers are under God's condemnation and are "by nature children of wrath" (Eph 2:3).

Man is not simply influenced by sin but is completely overpowered by it, and no one can escape that dominance by his own effort. Sin is a defiling disease that corrupts every person, degrades every individual, disquiets every soul. It steals peace and joy from the heart and replaces them with trouble and pain. Sin is implanted in every human life, and its deadly force brings a universal depravity that no man can cure.

Sin places men under the power of Satan, the ruler of the present world system (John 12:31). They are under the control of "the prince of the power of the air" and "of the spirit that is now working in the sons of disobedience" (Eph 2:2). As Paul went on to remind the Ephesian believers, all Christians were once a part of that evil system (v. 3). Jesus declared that Satan is the spiritual father of every unbeliever (John 8:41, 44), and that "the one who practices sin is of the devil; for the devil has sinned from the beginning" (1 John 3:8; cf. v. 10).

Because of sin, all of humankind is born in bondage to pain, disease, and death. One of Job's friends rightly observed that "Man is born for trouble, as sparks fly upward" (Job 5:7). Because of sin, all the rest of "creation was subjected to futility [and] ... groans and suffers the pains of childbirth together until now" (Rom 8:20, 22).

Because of sin, fallen men are heirs of God's judgment. "A certain terrifying expectation of judgment" awaits all unregenerate sinners, "and the fury of a fire which will consume [God's] adversaries" (Heb 10:27). The sinner who lives in unconcern apart from God does so as if he were Damocles at Dionysius's banquet, with a sword hanging over his neck by a single horsehair, which at any moment could break and usher him into eternity.

Because of sin, there is a curse on the sinner's soul. Among the last words Jesus spoke on earth were: "He who has disbelieved shall be condemned" (Mark 16:16). Paul declared, "If anyone does not love the Lord, let him be accursed" (1 Cor 16:22), and "For as many as are of the works of the Law are under a curse; for it is written, 'Cursed is everyone who does not abide by all things written in the book of the law, to perform them'" (Gal 3:10; cf. 2 Thess 1:8).

For at least three reasons, God is justified in His condemnation of sinners. First, He is justified because all men, through their lineage from Adam, share in the guilt of original sin and in the moral and spiritual depravity it produces. "For if by the transgression of the one, death reigned through the one," Paul has already explained in this epistle, "much more those who receive the abundance of grace and of the gift of righteousness will reign in life through the One, Jesus Christ. So then as through one transgression there resulted condemnation to all men, even so through one act of righteousness there resulted justification of life to all men" (Rom 5:17–18).

Second, God is justified in condemning sinners because every person is born with an evil nature. "Among them we too all formerly lived in the lusts of our flesh," Paul reminded the Ephesian believers, "indulging the desires of the flesh and of the mind, and were by nature children of wrath, even as the rest" (Eph 2:3).

Third, God is justified in condemning sinners because of the evil deeds their depraved natures inevitably produce. God "will render to every man according to his deeds: ... to those who are selfishly ambitious and do not obey the truth, but obey unrighteousness, wrath and indignation" (Rom 2:6, 8).

Because of sin, the unregenerate have no future to look forward to except eternal damnation in hell. That destiny is the sinner's second death, the lake of fire, judgment without mercy, pain without remission (Rev 20:14). The lost will be in a place of "outer darkness," Jesus said, where "there shall be weeping and gnashing of teeth" (Matt 8:12). As already noted, the Bible is an extremely condemnatory book, and the book of Romans is far from being an exception. Paul has already established that the entire human race, Jews as well as Gentiles, is depraved and under sin. He declares that "there is none righteous, not even one," that "there is none who seeks for God," that "there is none who does good," that "with their tongues they keep deceiving," that "destruction and misery are in their paths," and that "there is no fear of God before their eyes" (Rom 3:9–18).

Later in the epistle he declares that,

> Just as through one man sin entered into the world, and
> death through sin, and so death spread to all men, because all
> sinned.... And the gift is not like that which came through the
> one who sinned; for on the one hand the judgment arose from
> one transgression resulting in condemnation, but on the other
> hand the free gift arose from many transgressions resulting
> in justification.... So then as through one transgression there
> resulted condemnation to all men, even so through one act
> of righteousness there resulted justification of life to all men.
> (Rom 5:12, 16, 18)

Although God's revealed law is "holy and righteous
and good" (Rom 7:12) and is the standard by which men
are to live and be blessed, the unsaved have neither the
desire nor the ability to fulfill its demands. Because of
man's depraved and rebellious nature, the holy law of
God merely succeeds in arousing and aggravating the
sin that is already present (7:5).

In his second letter to Thessalonica, the apostle
reveals that "when the Lord Jesus shall be revealed from
heaven with His mighty angels in flaming fire, [He will
be] dealing out retribution to those who do not know
God and to those who do not obey the gospel of our
Lord Jesus. And these will pay the penalty of eternal
destruction, away from the presence of the Lord and
from the glory of His power" (2 Thess 1:7–9).

In itself, even the coming to earth of the Lord Jesus Christ, God incarnate, could not remove that condemnation. Jesus' perfect teaching and sinless life actually *increased* the condemnation of those who heard and saw Him. "And this is the judgment," Jesus said, "that the light is come into the world, and men loved the darkness rather than the light; for their deeds were evil. For everyone who does evil hates the light, and does not come to the light, lest his deeds should be exposed" (John 3:19–20). As the Lord had just explained, that was not God's desire: "For God did not send the Son into the world to judge the world, but that the world should be saved through Him" (John 3:17). But Christ's perfect teaching and perfect life had no more power in themselves to change men's hearts than had God's perfect law. Because Jesus' teaching was perfect and His living sinless, they demonstrated even more vividly than the law that fallen men cannot meet God's holy standards in their own power.

Such is the condition of every individual born into the world, and it is in light of that dreadful condition that Paul proclaims in Romans 8:1–4 the unspeakably wonderful truth about those who, by grace working through faith, belong to Jesus Christ. He proclaims to believers the thrilling promise that fills the heart with immeasurable consolation, joy, and hope. Some have called Romans 8:1 the most hopeful verse in Scripture. It is bewildering that any thinking mind or searching soul would not run with eagerness to receive such divine provision. But perhaps the greatest tragedy of sin is that it blinds the sinner to the life-giving promises of God and predisposes him to trust in the false and death-giving allurements of Satan.

In presenting God's salvation promise to believers, Paul focuses on its reality, no condemnation (v. l*a*); its reason, justification (vv. l*b*–2); its route, substitution (v. 3); and its result, sanctification (v. 4).

THE REALITY OF FREEDOM—
NO CONDEMNATION

There is therefore now no condemnation ... (8:1*a*)

By simple definition, **therefore** introduces a result, consequence, or conclusion based on what has been established previously. It seems unlikely that Paul is referring to the immediately preceding text. He has just finished lamenting the continued problem of sin in a believer's life, including his own. It is surely not on the basis of *that* truth that he confidently declares that believers are no longer under divine **condemnation.** One might expect rather that any further sin would deserve some sort of further judgment. But Paul makes clear that such is not the case with our gracious God. It seems probable that **therefore** marks a consequent conclusion from the entire first seven chapters, which focus primarily on justification by faith alone, made possible solely on the basis of and by the power of God's grace.

Accordingly, chapter 8 marks a major change in the focus and flow of the epistle. At this point the apostle begins to delineate the marvelous results of justification in the life of the believer. He begins by explaining, as best as possible to finite minds, some of the cardinal truths of salvation (no condemnation, as well as justification, substitution, and sanctification).

God's provision of salvation came not through Christ's perfect teaching or through His perfect life but through His perfect sacrifice on the cross. It is through Christ's death, not His life, that God provides the way of salvation. For those who place their trust in Christ and in what He has done on their behalf **there is therefore now no condemnation.**

The Greek word *katakrima* (**condemnation**) appears only in the book of Romans, here and in 5:16, 18. Although it relates to the sentencing for a crime, its primary focus is not so much on the verdict as on the penalty that the verdict demands. As Paul has already declared, the penalty, or **condemnation,** for sin is death (6:23).

Paul here announces the marvelous good news that for Christians there will be **no condemnation,** neither sentencing nor punishment for the sins that believers have committed or will ever commit.

Ouketi (**no**) is an emphatic negative adverb of time and carries the idea of complete cessation. In His parable about the king who forgave one of his slaves an overwhelming debt (Matt 18:23–27), Jesus pictured God's gracious and total forgiveness of the sins of those who come to Him in humble contrition and faith. That is the heart and soul of the gospel—that Jesus completely and permanently paid the debt of sin and the penalty of the law (which is **condemnation** to death) for every person who humbly asks for mercy and trusts in Him. Through the apostle John, God assures His children that "if anyone sins, we have an Advocate with the Father, Jesus Christ the righteous; and He Himself is the propitiation for our sins; and not for ours only, but also for those of the whole world" (1 John 2:1–2).

Jesus not only pays the believer's debt of sin but cleanses him "from all unrighteousness" (1 John 1:9). Still more amazingly, He graciously imputes and imparts to each believer His own perfect righteousness: "For by one offering He [Christ] has perfected for all time those who are sanctified" (Heb 10:14; cf. Rom 5:17; 2 Cor 5:21; Phil 3:9). More even than that, Jesus shares His vast heavenly inheritance with those who come to Him in faith (Eph 1:3, 11, 14). It is because of such immeasurable divine grace that Paul admonishes Christians to be continually "giving thanks to the Father, who has qualified us to share in the inheritance of the saints in light" (Col 1:12). Having been qualified by God the Father, we will never, under any circumstance, be subject to divine **condemnation.** How blessed to be placed beyond the reach of condemnation!

The truth that there can never be the eternal death penalty for believers is the foundation of the eighth chapter of Romans. As Paul asks rhetorically near the end of the chapter, "If God is for us, who is against us?" (v. 31), and again, "Who will bring a charge against God's elect? God is the one who justifies" (v. 33). If the highest tribunal in the universe justifies us, who can declare us guilty?

It is extremely important to realize that deliverance from condemnation is not based in the least measure on any form of perfection achieved by the believer. He does not attain the total eradication of sin during his earthly life. It is that truth that Paul establishes so intensely and poignantly in Romans 7. John declares that truth as unambiguously as possible in his first epistle: "If we say that we have no sin, we are deceiving ourselves, and the truth is not in us" (1 John 1:8). The Christian's conflict with sin does not end until he goes to be with the Lord. Nevertheless, there is still no condemnation—because the penalty for all the failures of his life has been paid in Christ and applied by grace.

It is also important to realize that deliverance from divine condemnation does not mean deliverance from divine discipline. "For those whom the Lord loves

He disciplines, and He scourges every son whom He receives" (Heb 12:6). Nor does deliverance from God's condemnation mean escape from our accountability to Him: "Do not be deceived, God is not mocked; for whatever a man sows, this he will also reap" (Gal 6:7).

THE REASON FOR FREEDOM— JUSTIFICATION

for those who are in Christ Jesus. For the law of the Spirit of life in Christ Jesus has set you free from the law of sin and of death. (8:1*b*–2)

As noted at the beginning of the previous section, the *therefore* that introduces verse 1 refers back to the major theme of the first seven chapters of the epistle—the believer's complete justification before God, graciously provided in response to trust in the sacrificial death and resurrection of His Son.

The divine condemnation from which believers are exonerated (8:1*a*) is without exception or qualification. It is bestowed on **those who are in Christ Jesus,** in other words, on every true Christian. Justification completely and forever releases every believer from sin's bondage and its penalty of death (6:23) and thereby fits him to stand sinless before a holy God forever. It is that particular aspect of justification on which Paul focuses at the beginning of chapter 8.

Paul's use of the first person singular pronouns (I and me) in 7:7–25 emphasizes the sad reality that, in this present life, no Christian, not even an apostle, is exempt from struggles with sin. In the opening verses of chapter 8, on the other hand, Paul emphasizes the marvelous reality that *every* believer, even the weakest and most unproductive, shares in complete and eternal freedom from sin's condemnation. The holiest of believers are warned that, although they are no longer under sin's slavish dominion, they will experience conflicts with it in this present life. And the weakest of believers are promised that, although they still stumble and fall into sin's power in their flesh, they will experience ultimate victory over sin in the life to come.

The key to every aspect of salvation is in the simple but infinitely profound phrase **in Christ Jesus.** A Christian is a person who is **in Christ Jesus.** Paul has already declared that "all of us who have been baptized into Christ Jesus have been baptized into His death," and that "therefore we have been buried with Him through baptism into death, in order that as Christ was raised from the dead through the glory of the Father, so we too might walk in newness of life. For if we have become united with Him in the likeness of His death, certainly we shall be also in the likeness of His resurrection" (Rom 6:3–5).

Being a Christian is not simply being outwardly identified with Christ but being *part* of Christ, not simply of being united with Him but united **in** Him. Our being in Christ is one of the profoundest of mysteries, which we will not fully understand until we meet Him face-to-face in heaven. But Scripture does shed light on that marvelous truth. We know that we are in Christ spiritually, in a divine and permanent union. "For as in Adam all die, so also in Christ all shall be made alive," Paul explains (1 Cor 15:22). Believers are also in Christ in a living, participatory sense. "Now you are Christ's body," Paul declares in that same epistle, "and individually members of it" (12:27). We are actually a part of Him and, in ways that are unfathomable to us now, we work when He works, grieve when He grieves, and rejoice when He rejoices. "For by one Spirit we were all baptized into one body," Paul assures us, "whether Jews or Greeks, whether slaves or free, and we were all made to drink of one Spirit" (1 Cor 12:13). Christ's own divine life pulses through us.

Many people are concerned about their family heritage, about who their ancestors were, where they lived, and what they did. For better or worse, we are all life-linked physically, intellectually, and culturally to our ancestors. In a similar, but infinitely more important way, we are linked to the family of God because of our relationship to His Son, Jesus Christ. It is for that reason that every Christian can say, "I have been crucified with Christ; and it is no longer I who live, but Christ lives in me; and the life which I now live in the flesh I live by faith in the Son of God, who loved me, and delivered Himself up for me" (Gal 2:20).

God's Word makes clear that every human being is a descendant of Adam and has inherited Adam's fallen nature. It makes just as clear that every true believer becomes a spiritual descendant of Jesus Christ, God's true Son, and is thereby adopted into the heavenly Father's own divine household as a beloved child. More than just being adopted, we inherit the very life of God in Christ.

Martin Luther said,

> It is impossible for a man to be a Christian without having Christ, and if he has Christ, he has at the same time all that is in Christ. What gives peace to the conscience is that by faith our sins are no more ours, but Christ's, upon whom God hath laid them all; and that, on the other hand, all Christ's righteousness is ours, to whom God hath given it. Christ lays His hand upon us, and we are healed. He casts His mantle upon us, and we are clothed; for He is the glorious Savior, blessed for ever. (Cited in Robert Haldane, *An Exposition of Romans* [MacDill AFB, Fla.: McDonald, 1958], p. 312)

The relationship between God and His chosen people Israel was beautifully illustrated in the garment of the high priest. Over his magnificent robes he wore a breastplate in which twelve different precious stones were embedded, representing the twelve tribes of Israel.

Each stone was engraved with the name of the tribe it represented. When the high priest entered the Holy of Holies once each year on the Day of Atonement, he stood before God with those visual representations of all His people.

That breastplate was a rich symbolism of Jesus Christ, our Great High Priest, standing before the Father making intercession on behalf of all those the Father has given Him (Heb 7:24–25). In what is commonly called His high priestly prayer, Jesus prayed on behalf of those who belong to Him "that they may all be one; even as Thou, Father, art in Me, and I in Thee, that they also may be in Us; that the world may believe that Thou didst send Me" (John 17:21).

Luther also wrote,

> Faith unites the soul with Christ as a spouse with her husband. Everything which Christ has becomes the property of the believing soul; everything which the soul has, becomes the property of Christ. Christ possesses all blessings and eternal life: they are thenceforward the property of the soul. The soul has all its iniquities and sins: they become thenceforward the property of Christ. It is then that a blessed exchange commences: Christ who is both God and man, Christ who has never sinned, and whose holiness is perfect, Christ the Almighty and Eternal, taking to Himself, by His nuptial ring of *faith*, all the sins of the believer, those sins are lost and abolished in Him; for no sins dwell before His infinite righteousness. Thus by faith the believer's soul is delivered from sins and clothed

with the eternal righteousness of her bridegroom Christ. (Cited in Haldane, *Exposition of Romans*, p. 313)

The phrase "who walk not after the flesh, but after the Spirit" appears at the end of verse 1 in the King James, but it is not found in the earliest manuscripts of Romans or in most modern translations. It is probable that a copyist inadvertently picked up the phrase from verse 4. Because the identical wording appears there, the meaning of the passage is not affected.

The conjunction **for,** which here carries the meaning of because, leads into the reason there is no condemnation for believers: **the law of the Spirit of life in Christ Jesus has set you free from the law of sin and of death.**

Paul does not here use the term **law** in reference to the Mosaic law or to other divine commandments or requirements. He uses it rather in the sense of a principle of operation, as he has done earlier in the letter, where he speaks of "a law of faith" (3:27) and as he does in Galatians, where he speaks of "the law of Christ" (6:2). Those who believe in Jesus Christ are delivered from the condemnation of a lower divine law, as it were, by submitting themselves to a higher divine law. The lower law is the divine principle in regard to **sin,** the penalty for which is **death,** and the higher law is **the law of the Spirit,** which bestows **life in Christ Jesus.**

But it should not be concluded that the **law** Paul is speaking of in this passage has no relationship to obedience. Obedience to God cannot save a person, because no person in his unredeemed sinfulness *wants* to obey God and could not obey perfectly even if he had the desire. But true salvation will always produce true obedience—never perfect in this life but nonetheless genuine and always present to some extent. When truly believed and received, the gospel of Jesus Christ always leads to the "obedience of faith" (Rom 16:25–26). The coming kingdom age of Christ that Jeremiah predicted and of which the writer of Hebrews refers is far from lawless. "For this is the covenant that I will make with the house of Israel after those days, says the Lord: I will put My laws into their minds, and I will write them upon their hearts" (Heb 8:10; cf. Jer 31:33). Release from the law's bondage and condemnation does not mean release from the law's requirements and standards. The higher law of the Spirit produces obedience to the lower law of duties.

The freedom that Christ gives is complete and permanent deliverance from sin's power and penalty (and ultimately from its presence). It also gives the ability to obey God. The very notion of a Christian who is free to do as he pleases is self-contradictory. A person who believes that salvation leads from law to license does not have the least understanding of the gospel of grace and can make no claim on Christ's saviorhood and certainly no claim on His lordship.

In speaking of **the Spirit of life in Christ Jesus,** Paul makes unambiguous later in this chapter that he is referring to the Holy **Spirit.** The Christian's mind is set on the things of the Spirit (v. 6) and is indwelt and given life by the Holy Spirit (vv. 9–11). Paul summarized the working of those two laws earlier in the epistle: "For the wages of sin is death, but the free gift of God is eternal life in Christ Jesus our Lord" (Rom 6:23).

When Jesus explained the way of salvation to Nicodemus, He said, "Unless one is born of water and the Spirit, he cannot enter into the kingdom of God" (John 3:5). God "saved us, not on the basis of deeds which we have done in righteousness," Paul explains, "but according to His mercy, by the washing of regeneration and renewing by the Holy Spirit, whom He poured out upon us richly through Jesus Christ our Savior" (Titus 3:5–6). It is the Holy **Spirit** who bestows and energizes spiritual **life** in the person who places his trust **in Christ Jesus.** Paul could not be talking of any spirit but the Holy Spirit, because only God's Holy Spirit can bring spiritual life to a heart that is spiritually dead.

The truths of Romans 7 are among the most depressing and heartrending in all of Scripture, and it is largely for that reason that many interpreters believe they cannot describe a Christian. But Paul was simply being honest and candid about the frustrating and discouraging spiritual battles that every believer faces. It is, in fact, the most faithful and obedient Christian who faces the greatest spiritual struggles. Just as in physical warfare, it is those on the front lines who encounter the enemy's most fierce attacks. But just as frontline battle can reveal courage, it can also reveal weaknesses and vulnerability. Even the most valiant soldier is subject to injury and discouragement.

During his earthly life, the Christian will always have residual weaknesses from his old humanness, the old fleshly person he used to be. No matter how closely he walks with the Lord, he is not yet completely free from sin's power. That is the discomfiting reality of Romans 7.

But the Christian is no longer a slave to sin as he once was, no longer under sin's total domination and control. Now he is free from sin's bondage and its ultimate penalty. Satan, the world, and his own humanness still can cause him to stumble and falter, but they can no longer control or destroy him, because his new life in Christ is the very divine life of God's own Spirit. That is the comforting truth of Romans 8.

The story is told of a man who operated a drawbridge. At a certain time each afternoon, he had to raise the bridge for a ferry boat and then lower it quickly for a passenger train that crossed at high speed a few minutes later. One day the man's young son was visiting his father at work and decided to go down below to get a better look at the ferry as it passed. Fascinated by the sight, he did not watch carefully where he was going and fell into the giant gears. One foot became caught and the boy was helpless to free himself. The father saw what happened but knew that if he took time to extricate his son, the train would plunge into the river before the bridge could be lowered. But if he lowered the bridge to save the hundreds of passengers and crew members on the train, his son would be crushed to death. When he heard the train's whistle, indicating it would soon reach the river, he knew what he had to do. His son was very dear to him, whereas all the people on the train were total strangers. The sacrifice of his son for the sake of the other people was an act of pure grace and mercy.

That story portrays something of the infinitely greater sacrifice God the Father made when He sent His only beloved Son to earth to die for the sins of mankind—to whom He owed nothing but condemnation.

THE ROUTE TO FREEDOM—SUBSTITUTION

For what the Law could not do, weak as it was through the flesh, God did: sending His own Son in the likeness of sinful flesh and as an offering for sin, He condemned sin in the flesh ... (8:3)

This verse is perhaps the most definitive and succinct statement of the substitutionary atonement to be found in Scripture. It expresses the heart of the gospel message, the wondrous truth that Jesus Christ paid the penalty on behalf of every person who would turn from sin and trust in Him as Lord and Savior.

As in the previous verse, the conjunction **for** carries the meaning of because and gives an explanation for what has just been stated. Believers are set free from the law of sin and death and are made alive by the law of the Spirit of life because of what Jesus Christ has done for them.

The Law can provoke sin in men and condemn them for it, but it cannot save them from its penalty. "For as many as are of the works of the Law are under a curse," Paul explained to the Galatians, "for it is written, 'Cursed is everyone who does not abide by all things written in the book of the law, to perform them'" (Gal 3:10). Later in that same chapter he says: "Is the Law then contrary to the promises of God? May it never be! For if a law had been given which was able to impart life, then righteousness would indeed have been based on law" (3:21). God's holy law can only set forth the standards of His righteousness and show men how utterly incapable they are in themselves of fulfilling those standards.

Paul has already explained that "this commandment [i.e., the law, v. 9], which was to result in life [if obeyed], proved to result in death for me; for sin, taking opportunity through the commandment, deceived me, and through it killed me" (Rom 7:10–11). When God created man, sin had no place in His creation. But when man fell, the alien power of sin corrupted his very being and condemned him to death, both physical and spiritual. The whole human race was placed under the curse of God. Sin consigned fallen mankind to a divine debtor's prison, as it were, and the law became his jailer. The law, given as the standard for living under divine blessing and joy, became a killer.

Although it is "holy and righteous and good" (Rom 7:12), **the Law could not** save men from sin because it was **weak ... through the flesh.** The sinful corruption of **the flesh** made **the Law** powerless to save men. The law cannot make men righteous but can only expose their unrighteousness and condemn them for it. The law cannot make men perfect but can only reveal their great imperfection. As Paul explained in the synagogue at Antioch of Pisidia, through Jesus Christ "forgiveness of sins is proclaimed to you, and through Him everyone who believes is freed from all things, from which you could not be freed through the Law of Moses" (Acts 13:38–39).

During His incarnation, Jesus was the embodiment of the law of Moses. He alone of all men who have ever lived or will ever live perfectly fulfilled the law of God. "Do not think that I came to abolish the Law or the

Prophets," He said; "I did not come to abolish, but to fulfill" (Matt 5:17). During one of His discourses in the Temple, Jesus exposed the sinfulness of the self-righteous scribes and Pharisees, who, by their failure to throw stones at the woman taken in adultery, admitted they were not without sin (John 8:7–9). Later on that same occasion Jesus challenged His enemies to convict Him of any sin, and no one could do so or even tried (v. 46).

Some people, including many professing Christians, believe that they can achieve moral and spiritual perfection by living up to God's standards by their own power. But James reminds us that "whoever keeps the whole law and yet stumbles in one point, he has become guilty of all" (Jas 2:10). In other words, even a single sin, no matter how small and no matter when committed, is sufficient to disqualify a person for heaven.

On one occasion a young man came to Jesus and said to Him,

> "Teacher, what good thing shall I do that I may obtain eternal life?" And He said to him, "Why are you asking Me about what is good? There is only One who is good; but if you wish to enter into life, keep the commandments." He said to Him, "Which ones?" And Jesus said, "You shall not commit murder; you shall not commit adultery; you shall not steal; you shall not bear false witness; honor your father and mother; and you shall love your neighbor as yourself." The young man said to

Him, "All these things I have kept; what am I still lacking?" Jesus said to him, "If you wish to be complete, go and sell your possessions and give to the poor, and you shall have treasure in heaven; and come, follow Me." But when the young man heard this statement, he went away grieved; for he was one who owned much property. (Matt 19:16–22)

This man was extremely religious. But he demonstrated that, despite his diligence in obeying the commandments, he failed to keep the two greatest commandments—to "love the Lord your God with all your heart, and with all your soul, and with all your mind" and to "'love your neighbor as yourself.' On these two commandments," Jesus went on to say, "depend the whole Law and the Prophets" (Matt 22:37–40). The young man who came to Jesus was self-centered, selfish, and materialistic. His love for himself surpassed his love for God and for his fellow man. Consequently, his meticulous religious living counted for absolutely nothing before God.

God's law commands righteousness, but it cannot provide the means to achieve that righteousness. Therefore, what the law was unable to do for fallen man, **God** Himself **did.** The law can condemn the sinner, but only God can condemn and destroy sin, and that is what He has done on behalf of those who trust in His Son—by His coming to earth **in the likeness of sinful flesh and as an offering for sin.**

Jesus said, "I am the living bread that came down out of heaven; if anyone eats of this bread, he shall live forever; and the bread also which I shall give for the life of the world is My flesh" (John 6:51). In His incarnation Jesus was completely a man, fully incarnated. But He was only **in the likeness of,** in the outward appearance of, **sinful flesh.** Although Paul does not here specifically mention Jesus' sinlessness, his phrasing carefully guards that profound truth.

Jesus was "tempted in all things as we are, yet without sin" (Heb 4:15). If He had not been both fully human and fully sinless, He could not have offered an acceptable sacrifice to God for the sins of the world. If Jesus had not Himself been without sin, He not only could not have made a sacrifice for fallen mankind but would have needed to have a sacrifice made on His own behalf. Jesus resisted every temptation of Satan and denied sin any part in His earthly life. Sin was compelled to yield its supremacy in the **flesh** to the Victor, whereby Jesus Christ became sovereign over sin and its consequence, death.

Those who trust in Christ not only are saved from the penalty of sin but also are able for the first time to fulfill God's righteous standards. The flesh of a believer is still weak and subject to sin, but the inner person is remade in the image of Christ and has the power through His Spirit to resist and overcome sin. No Christian will be perfected during his earthly life, but he has no excuse for sinning, because he has God's own power to resist sin. John assures believers that "greater is He [the Holy Spirit] who is in you than he [Satan] who is in the world" (1 John 4:4). As Paul has already declared, "For if while we were enemies, we were reconciled to God through the death of His Son, much more, having been reconciled, we shall be saved by His life," that is, be kept saved and protected from sin's domination (Rom 5:10).

Speaking of His impending crucifixion, Jesus said, "Now judgment is upon this world; now the ruler of this world shall be cast out" (John 12:31). In other words, by His death on the cross Christ condemned and conquered both sin and Satan. He bore the fury of God's wrath on all sin, and in doing so broke sin's power over those whose trust is in His giving of Himself **as an offering for sin** on their behalf. By trusting in Jesus Christ, those who formerly were children of Satan become children of God, those who were targets of God's wrath become recipients of His grace. On the cross Jesus broke sin's power and assigned sin to its final destruction. God "made Him who knew no sin to be sin on our behalf, that we might become the righteousness of God in Him" (2 Cor 5:21). Christ was "offered once to bear the sins of many" (Heb 9:28).

Jesus' teaching, miracles, and sinless life were of great importance in His earthly ministry. But His supreme purpose in coming to earth was to be **an**

offering for sin. Without the sacrifice of Himself for the sins of the world, everything else Jesus did would have left men in their sins, still separated from God.

To teach that men can live a good life by following Jesus' example is patronizing foolishness. To try to follow Jesus' perfect example without having His own life and Spirit within us is even more impossible and frustrating than trying to fulfill the Mosaic law. Jesus' example cannot save us but instead further demonstrates the impossibility of saving ourselves by our own efforts at righteousness.

The only hope men have for salvation from their sin is in their trust in the **offering for sin** that Christ Himself made at Calvary. And when He became that **offering,** He took upon Himself the penalty of death for the sins of all mankind. In his commentary on Romans, the nineteenth-century Scottish evangelist Robert Haldane wrote, "We see the Father assume the place of judge against His Son, in order to become the Father of those who were His enemies. The Father condemns the Son of His love, that He may absolve the children of wrath" (*Expostion of Romans*, p. 324).

Jesus Christ **condemned sin in the flesh.** Whereas sin once condemned the believer, now Christ his Savior condemns sin, delivering the believer from sin's power and penalty. The law condemns sin in the sense of exposing it for what it really is and in the sense of declaring its penalty of death. But the law is unable to condemn sin in the sense of delivering a sinner from his sinfulness or in the sense of overpowering sin and consigning it to its ultimate destruction. Only the Lord Jesus Christ was able to do that, and it is that amazing truth that inspired Paul to exult, "'O death, where is your victory? O death, where is your sting?' The sting of death is sin, and the power of sin is the law; but thanks be to God, who gives us the victory through our Lord Jesus Christ" (1 Cor 15:55–57).

The prophet Isaiah eloquently predicted the sacrifice of the incarnate Christ, saying,

> Surely our griefs He Himself bore, and our sorrows He carried; Yet we ourselves esteemed Him stricken, smitten of God, and afflicted. But He was pierced through for our transgressions, He was crushed for our iniquities; the chastening for our well-being fell upon Him, and by His scourging we are healed. All of us like sheep have gone astray, each of us has turned to his own way; but the Lord has caused the iniquity of us all to fall on Him. He was oppressed and He was afflicted, yet He did not open His mouth; like a lamb that is led to slaughter, and like a sheep that is silent before its shearers, so He did not open His mouth. By oppression and judgment He was taken away; and as for His generation, who considered that He was cut off out of the land of the living, for the transgression of my people to whom the stroke was due? (Isa 53:4–8)

THE RESULT OF FREEDOM—SANCTIFICATION

in order that the requirement of the Law might be fulfilled in us, who do not walk according to the flesh, but according to the Spirit. (8:4)

The believer's freedom from sin results in his present as well as in his ultimate sanctification. The true Christian has both the desire and the divinely imparted ability to live righteously while he is still on earth. Because God sent His own Son to redeem mankind by providing the only sacrifice that can condemn and remove their sin (v. 3), **the requirement of the Law** is able **to be fulfilled in us,** that is, in believers.

Paul obviously is not speaking here of the justifying work of salvation but of its sanctifying work, its being lived out in the believer's earthly life. Apart from the working of the Holy Spirit through the life of a redeemed person, human efforts at righteousness are as contaminated and useless as filthy garments (Isa 64:6). But because the Christian has been cleansed of sin and been given God's own divine nature within him, he now longs for and is able to live a life of holiness.

God does not free men from their sin in order for them to do as they please but to do as He pleases. God does not redeem men in order that they may continue sinning but **in order that** they may begin to live righteously by having **the requirement of the Law ... fulfilled in** them.

Because they are no longer under law but are now under grace, some Christians claim that it makes little difference what they do, because just as nothing they could have done could have saved them, so nothing they now do can cause them to lose their salvation. But the Holy Spirit could never prompt a Christian to make such a foolish and ungodly statement. The spiritual Christian knows that God's law is holy, righteous, and good (Rom 7:12) and that he has been saved in order to have that divine holiness, righteousness, and goodness **fulfilled** in him. And that is his desire. He has holy longings.

The phrase **who do not walk according to the flesh, but according to the Spirit** is not an admonition but a statement of fact that applies to all believers. As Paul explains several verses later, no person who belongs to Christ is without the indwelling Holy Spirit (v. 9). Being indwelt by the Spirit is not a mark of special maturity or spirituality but the mark of every true Christian, without exception.

In its figurative sense, *peripateō* (to **walk**) refers to an habitual way or bent of life, to a life-style. Luke describes Zacharias and Elizabeth, the parents of John the Baptist, as being "righteous in the sight of God, walking blamelessly in all the commandments and requirements of the Lord" (Luke 1:6). Paul counseled the Ephesian believers to "walk no longer just as the Gentiles also walk, in the futility of their mind" (Eph

4:17). John declares that, "if we walk in the light as [God] Himself is in the light, we have fellowship with one another, and the blood of Jesus His Son cleanses us from all sin" (1 John 1:7).

Paul asserts that a true believer—whether young or old, immature or mature, well taught or poorly taught—does **not walk according to the flesh.** Just as categorically he declares that a true believer does walk **according to the Spirit.** There are no exceptions. Because every true believer is indwelt by the Spirit, every true believer will produce the fruit of the Spirit (Gal 5:22–23). Jesus made clear "that unless your righteousness surpasses that of the scribes and Pharisees, you shall not enter the kingdom of heaven" (Matt 5:20). At the end of that first chapter of the Sermon on the Mount, Jesus commanded, "You are to be perfect as your heavenly Father is perfect" (5:48).

Nothing is dearer to God's heart than the moral and spiritual excellence of those He has created in His own image—and nothing is dearer to them. He does not want them to have only imputed righteousness but practical righteousness as well. And that also is what they want. It is practical righteousness about which Paul speaks here, just as he does in the opening words of his letter to the church at Ephesus: "[God] chose us in [Christ] before the foundation of the world, that we should be holy and blameless before Him" (Eph 1:4).

It is God's great desire that believers live out the perfect righteousness that He reckons to them when they are saved—that they live like His children and no longer like the children of the world and of Satan. Positional righteousness is to be reflected in practical righteousness. Christ does not want a bride who is only positionally righteous but one who is actually righteous, just as He Himself is righteous. And through His indwelling Spirit, He gives believers that desire.

The purpose of the gospel is not to make men happy but to make them holy. As the Beatitudes make clear, genuine happiness comes to those who belong to Christ and are obedient to His will. But true happiness comes only from holiness. God promises happiness, but He demands holiness, without which "no one will see the Lord" (Heb 12:14).

In his book titled *God's Righteous Kingdom*, Walter J. Chantry writes,

> When preachers speak as if God's chief desire is for men to be happy, then multitudes with problems flock to Jesus. Those who have ill-health, marital troubles, financial frustration, and loneliness look to our Lord for the desires of their hearts. Each conceives of joy as being found in health, peace, prosperity or companionship. But in search of illusive happiness they are not savingly joined to Jesus Christ. Unless men will be holy, God is determined that they shall be forever miserable and damned. (Carlisle, PA: Banner of Truth, 1980, p. 67)

Righteousness is the very heart of salvation. It is for righteousness that God saves those who trust in His Son. "For I am not ashamed of the gospel," Paul declared at the beginning of the Roman epistle, "for in it the righteousness of God is revealed from faith to faith; as it is written, 'But the righteous man shall live by faith'" (Rom 1:16–17). Peter admonishes believers, "Like the Holy One who called you, be holy yourselves also in all your behavior" (1 Pet 1:15). Practical righteousness leads believers "to deny ungodliness and worldly desires and to live sensibly, righteously and godly in the present age" (Titus 2:11–12; cf. Gal 5:24–25). As Augustine observed many centuries ago, grace was given for one reason, that the law might be fulfilled.

When a sinner leaves the courts of God and has received a pardon for sin by virtue of Christ's sacrifice, the work of God in his life has just begun. As the believer leaves the courtroom, as it were, God hands him the code of life and says, "Now you have in you My Spirit, whose power will enable you to fulfill My law's otherwise impossible demands."

Scripture is clear that, in some mystical way known only to God, a person begins to walk by the Spirit the moment he believes. But, on the other hand, he is also admonished to walk by the Spirit as he lives out his earthly life under the lordship of Christ and in the power of the Spirit. As with salvation itself, walking by the Spirit comes first of all by God's sovereign work in the believer's heart, but it also involves the exercise of the believer's will. Romans 8:4 is speaking of the first, whereas Galatians 5:25 ("let us ... walk by the Spirit") is speaking of the second.

As far as a Christian's life is concerned, everything that is a spiritual reality is also a spiritual responsibility. A genuine Christian *will* commune with his heavenly Father in prayer, but he also has the responsibility to pray. A Christian *is* taught by the Holy Spirit, but he is also obligated to seek the Spirit's guidance and help. The Holy Spirit *will* produce spiritual fruit in a believer's life, but the believer is also admonished to bear fruit. Those truths are part of the amazing and seemingly paradoxical tension between God's sovereignty and man's will. Although man's mind is incapable of understanding such mysteries, the believer accepts them because they are clearly taught in God's Word.

We know little of the relationship between God and Adam before the Fall, except that it was direct and intimate. The Lord had given but one command, a command that was given for Adam and Eve's own good and that was easily obeyed. Until that one command was transgressed, they lived naturally in the perfect will of God. Doing His will was part of their very being.

The believer's relationship to God is much like that. Although Christians are drawn back to the old ways by the fleshly remnants of their life before salvation, their new being makes obedience to God the "natural" thing to do.

The Christian's obligations to God are not another form of legalism. The person who is genuinely saved has a new and divine nature that is, by definition, attuned to God's will. When he lives by his new nature in the power of the Spirit, his desire is God's desire, and no compulsion is involved. But because the believer is still clothed in the old self, he sometimes resists God's will. It is only when he goes against God's will and against his own new nature that the divine commands and standards seem burdensome. On the other hand, the faithful child of God who is obedient from the heart can always say with the psalmist, "O how I love Thy law!" (Ps 119:97).

02

LIFE IN THE SPIRIT—PART 2 THE SPIRIT CHANGES OUR NATURE AND EMPOWERS US FOR VICTORY

ROMANS 8:5–13

For those who are according to the flesh set their minds on the things of the flesh, but those who are according to the Spirit, the things of the Spirit. For the mind set on the flesh is death, but the mind set on the Spirit is life and peace, because the mind set on the flesh is hostile toward God; for it does not subject itself to the law of God, for it is not even able to do so; and those who are in the flesh cannot please God. However, you are not in the flesh but in the Spirit, if indeed the Spirit of God dwells in you. But if anyone does not have the Spirit of Christ, he does not belong to Him. And if Christ is in you, though the body is dead because of sin, yet the spirit is alive because of righteousness. But if the Spirit of Him who raised Jesus from the dead dwells in you, He who raised Christ Jesus from the dead will also give life to your mortal bodies through His Spirit who indwells you.

So then, brethren, we are under obligation, not to the flesh, to live according to the flesh—for if you are living according to the flesh, you must die; but if by the Spirit you are putting to death the deeds of the body, you will live. (8:5–13)

The spiritual richness, both theological and practical, of this chapter is beyond calculation and surpasses adequate comment. When read by a believer with an open mind and an obedient heart, it is incredibly enriching. It is one of the supreme life-changing chapters in Scripture. It moves along in an ever-ascending course, concluding in the marvelous paean of praise and assurance: "For I am convinced that neither death, nor life, nor angels, nor principalities, nor things present, nor things to come, nor powers, nor height, nor depth, nor any other created thing, shall be able to separate us from the love of God, which is in Christ Jesus our Lord" (Rom 8:38–39).

The Holy Spirit is mentioned but once in the first seven chapters of Romans, but is referred to nearly twenty times in chapter 8. The Spirit is to a believer what God the Creator is to the physical world. Without God, the physical world would not exist. It has been created and is continually sustained by the omnipotent power of God. So the Holy Spirit—who also, of course, participated in the creation of the world—is to the Christian. The Holy Spirit is the divine agent who creates, sustains, and preserves spiritual life in those who place their trust in Jesus Christ. It is the Holy Spirit who ultimately will bring every believer into the full consummation of his salvation by granting him eternal glory in the presence of God.

It should be made clear that the Holy Spirit is not merely an influence or an impersonal power emanating from God. He is a person, the third member of the Trinity, equal in every way to God the Father and God the Son. The doctrine of God's being one essence, yet existing in three persons, is one of the most certain truths in Scripture. Yet the Holy Spirit is often not respected as every bit as much a divine person as the Father and the Son.

Among the many characteristics of personhood that the Holy Spirit possesses and manifests are: He functions with mind, emotion, and will; He loves the saints, He communicates with them, teaches, guides, comforts, and chastises them; He can be grieved, quenched, lied to, tested, resisted, and blasphemed. The Bible speaks of His omniscience, His omnipotence, His omnipresence, and His divine glory and holiness. He is called God, Lord, the Spirit of God, the Spirit of the Lord, the Spirit of Yahweh (or Jehovah), the Spirit of the Father, the Spirit of the Son, the Spirit of Jesus, and the Comforter and Advocate for believers.

Scripture reveals that the Holy Spirit was fully active with the Father and Son in the creation and that He has been with all believers and enabled and empowered them even before Pentecost. He has always been convicting men of sin, giving salvation to those who truly believed, and teaching them to worship, obey, and serve God rightly. The Holy Spirit has been the divine agent who uniquely came upon God's servants and inspired God's sovereignly chosen men to pen God's Word. True believers have always served God not by human might or power but by the Holy Spirit (cf. Zech 4:6). The Spirit was involved in Jesus' conception as a human being and in Jesus' baptism, anointing, temptation, teaching, miracles, death, and resurrection.

Since Pentecost, the Holy Spirit has, in His fulness, indwelt all believers, illuminating their understanding and application of God's Word as well as empowering them for sanctification in a greater way than had ever occurred before. He fills them, seals them, communes with them, fellowships with them, intercedes for them, comforts them, admonishes them, sanctifies them, and enables them to resist sin and to serve God.

In the present passage (Rom 8:5–13), Paul continues to disclose the innumerable results of justification, specifically the marvelous, Spirit-wrought benefits of freedom from condemnation. In verses 2–3 he has discussed the Spirit's freeing us from sin and death, and in verse 4 His enabling us to fulfill God's law. In verses 5–13 Paul reveals that the Spirit also changes our nature and grants us strength for victory over the unredeemed flesh.

THE HOLY SPIRIT CHANGES OUR NATURE

For those who are according to the flesh set their minds on the things of the flesh, but those who are according to the Spirit, the things of the Spirit. For the mind set on the flesh is death, but the mind set on the Spirit is life and peace, because the mind set

on the flesh is hostile toward God; for it does not subject itself to the law of God, for it is not even able to do so; and those who are in the flesh cannot please God. However, you are not in the flesh but in the Spirit, if indeed the Spirit of God dwells in you. But if anyone does not have the Spirit of Christ, he does not belong to Him. And if Christ is in you, though the body is dead because of sin, yet the spirit is alive because of righteousness. But if the Spirit of Him who raised Jesus from the dead dwells in you, He who raised Christ Jesus from the dead will also give life to your mortal bodies through His Spirit who indwells you. (8:5–11)

In verse 4 Paul speaks of the believer's behavior, contending that he does "not walk according to the flesh, but according to the Spirit." As in verses 2 and 3, the conjunction **for** in verse 5 carries the meaning of because. The point is that a believer does not behave according to the flesh because his new heart and mind are no longer centered on the things of the flesh and ruled by sin.

In God's eyes, there are only two kinds of people in the world, those who do not belong to Him and those who do. Put another way, there are only **those who are according to the flesh** and **those who are according to the Spirit.** As far as spiritual life is concerned, God takes no consideration of gender, age, education, talent, class, race, or any other human distinctions (Gal 3:28). He differentiates people solely on the basis of their relationship to Him, and the difference is absolute.

Obviously there are degrees in both categories. Some unsaved people exhibit high moral behavior, and, on the other hand, many saints do not mind the things of God as obediently as they should. But every human being is completely in one spiritual state of being or the other; he either belongs to God or he does not. Just as a person cannot be partly dead and partly alive physically, neither can he be partly dead and partly alive spiritually. There is no middle ground. A person is either forgiven and in the kingdom of God or unforgiven and in the kingdom of this world. He is either a child of God or a child of Satan.

In this context, the phrase **according to** refers to basic spiritual nature. The Greek could be translated literally as **those** *being* **according to,** indicating a person's fundamental essence, bent, or disposition. **Those who are according to the flesh** are the unsaved, the unforgiven, the unredeemed, the unregenerate. **Those who are according to the Spirit** are the saved, the forgiven, the redeemed, the regenerated children of God. As the apostle points out a few verses later, the unsaved not only are according to the flesh but are in the flesh and are *not* indwelt by the Holy Spirit. The saved, on the other hand, not only are according to the Spirit but are *in* the Spirit and *indwelt* by Him

(v. 9). Here in verse 5 Paul is speaking of the determinant spiritual *pattern* of a person's life, whereas in verses 8–9 he is speaking of the spiritual *sphere* of a person's life.

Phroneō, the verb behind **set their minds,** refers to the basic orientation, bent, and thought patterns of the mind, rather than to the mind or intellect itself (Greek *nous*). It includes a person's affections and will as well as his reasoning. Paul uses the same verb in Philippians, where he admonishes believers to "have this attitude [or, "mind"] in yourselves which was also in Christ Jesus" (2:5; see also 2:2; 3:15, 19; Col 3:2).

The basic disposition of the unredeemed is to "indulge the flesh in its corrupt desires" (2 Pet 2:10). The lost are those "whose end is destruction, whose god is their appetite, and whose glory is in their shame, who set their minds on earthly things" (Phil 3:19). **The things of the flesh** includes false philosophies and religions, which invariably appeal, whether overtly or subtly, to **the flesh** through self-interest and self-effort.

But those who are according to the Spirit, Paul says, set their minds on **the things of the Spirit.** In other words, those who belong to God are concerned about godly things. As Jonathan Edwards liked to say, they have "holy affections," deep longings after God and sanctification. As Paul has made clear in Romans 7, even God's children sometimes falter in their obedience to Him. But as the apostle said of himself, they nevertheless "joyfully concur with the law of God in the inner man" (Rom 7:22). Despite their many spiritual failures, their basic orientation and innermost concerns have to do with **the things of the Spirit.**

Phronēma (**the mind**) is the noun form of the verb in verse 5, and, like the verb, refers to the content or thought patterns of the mind rather than to the mind itself. It is significant that Paul does not say that **the mind set on the flesh** *leads* to **death,** but that it is death. The unsaved person is already dead spiritually. The apostle is stating a spiritual equation, not a spiritual consequence. The consequence involved in this relationship is the reverse: that is, because unredeemed men are already spiritually dead, their minds are inevitably **set on the flesh.** Paul reminded the Ephesian believers that, before salvation, they were all once "dead in [their] trespasses and sins" (Eph 2:1).

There is, of course, a sense in which sin *leads* to death. "But your iniquities have made a separation between you and your God," Isaiah declared to Israel, "and your sins have hidden His face from you, so that He does not hear" (Isa 59:2). Earlier in the book of Romans Paul explained that "the wages of sin is death" (6:23) and that "while we were in the flesh, the sinful passions, which were aroused by the Law, were at work in the members of our body to bear fruit for death" (7:5; cf. Gal 6:8).

But Paul's emphasis in the present passage is on

the state of death in which every unbeliever already exists, even while his body and mind may be very much alive and active. "A natural man does not accept the things of the Spirit of God," Paul explained to the Corinthian believers, "for they are foolishness to him, and he cannot understand them, because they are spiritually appraised" (1 Cor 2:14).

Some years ago I conducted the funeral for a baby girl killed in an automobile accident. Before the service the mother kept reaching into the casket, taking the lifeless little body in her arms and caressing her and crying softly to her. The baby, of course, could no longer respond to anything in the physical realm, because there was no life there to respond.

The unsaved person is a spiritual corpse and consequently is completely unable, in himself, to respond to the things of God. Unless the Holy Spirit intervenes by convicting him of sin and enabling him to respond to God by faith and thus being made alive, the unsaved person is as insensitive to the things of God as that baby was to the caresses and cries of her mother.

But the mind set on the Spirit is life and peace. Again Paul states an equation, not a consequence. **The mind set on the Spirit,** that is, on the things of God, equates **life and peace,** which equates being a Christian. **The mind set on the Spirit** is synonymous with Christian, a person who has been born again, given spiritual **life** by God's grace working through his faith.

The mind set on the Spirit is also synonymous with spiritual **peace,** that is, peace with God. The unsaved person, no matter how much he may claim to honor, worship, and love God, is God's enemy—a truth Paul has already pointed out in this epistle. Before we were saved, he states, we were all enemies of God (5:10). Only the person who has new **life** in God has **peace** with God.

The obvious corollary of that truth is that it is impossible to have a **mind set on the Spirit,** which includes having spiritual **life and peace,** and yet remain dead to the things of God. A professing Christian who has no sensitivity to the things of God, no "holy affections," does not belong to God. Nor does a merely professing Christian have a battle with the flesh, because he is, in reality, still naturally inclined toward the things of the flesh. He longs for the things of the flesh, which are normal to him, because he is still in the flesh and has his mind wholly set on the things of the flesh.

An unbeliever may be deeply concerned about not living up to the religious standards and code he has set for himself or that his denomination or other religious organization has set, and he may struggle hard in trying to achieve those goals. But his struggle is purely on a human level. It is a struggle not generated by the love of God but by self-love and the subsequent desire to gain greater favor with God or men on the basis of superior personal achievement. Whatever religious and moral struggles he may have are problems of flesh with flesh, not of Spirit against flesh, because the Holy Spirit is not in a fleshly person and a fleshly person is not in the Spirit.

As Paul has illustrated from his own life in Romans 7, a true Christian battles with the flesh because his mortal body still hangs on and tries to lure him back into the old sinful ways. But he is no longer *in* the flesh but *in* the Spirit. Speaking of true believers, Paul said, "For the flesh sets its desire against the Spirit, and the Spirit against the flesh; for these are in opposition to one another, so that you may not do the things that you please" (Gal 5:17). But "if we live by the Spirit," he goes on to say, "let us also walk by the Spirit" (v. 25; cf. v. 16). In other words, because a believer's new nature is divine and is indwelt by God's own Spirit, he desires to behave accordingly.

It is important to note that, when he speaks of sin in a Christian's life, Paul is always careful to identify sin with the outer, corrupted body, not with the new, inner nature. A believer's flesh is not redeemed when he trusts in Christ. If that were so, all Christians would immediately become perfect when they are saved, which even apart from the testimony of Scripture is obviously not true. The sinful vestige of unredeemed humanness will not fall away until the Christian goes to be with the Lord. It is for that reason that the New Testament sometimes speaks of a Christian's salvation in the future tense (see Rom 13:11). Referring to those who were already saved, Paul says later in this chapter, "Having the first fruits of the Spirit, even we ourselves groan within ourselves, waiting eagerly for our adoption as sons, the redemption of our body" (Rom 8:23). As the apostle explains to the Corinthians, "It is sown a perishable body it is raised an imperishable body; it is sown in dishonor, it is raised in glory; it is sown in weakness, it is raised in power; it is sown a natural body it is raised a spiritual body. If there is a natural body there is also a spiritual body" (1 Cor 15:42–44).

No matter how self-sacrificing, moral, and sincere the life of an unredeemed person may be, his religious efforts are selfish because he cannot truly serve God, **because** his **mind** is **set on the flesh.** Paul again (cf. v. 6) uses the term *phronēma* (**the mind**), which refers to the content, the thought patterns, the basic inclination and orientation of a person. This inclination, or bent, of **the flesh** is even more deep-seated and significant than actual disobedience, which is simply the outward manifestation of the inner, fleshly compulsions of an unregenerate person.

Every unredeemed person, whether religious or atheistic, whether outwardly moral or outwardly wicked, **is hostile toward God.** An unsaved person cannot live a godly and righteous life because he has no godly and righteous nature or resources. He therefore *cannot* have genuine love for God or for the things of God. His sinful, fleshly mind **does not subject itself to the law of God, for it is not even able to do so.** Even an unbeliever whose life seems to be a model of good works is not capable of doing anything truly good, because he is not motivated or empowered by God and because his works are produced by the flesh for self-centered reasons and can never be to God's glory. It clearly follows, then, that if the fleshly mind does not and cannot subject itself to the law of God, **those who are in the flesh cannot please God.**

Men were created for the very purpose of pleasing God. At the beginning of the practical section of this epistle Paul says, "I urge you therefore, brethren, by the mercies of God, to present your bodies a living and holy sacrifice, acceptable to God, which is your spiritual service of worship. And do not be conformed to this world, but be transformed by the renewing of your mind, that you may prove what the will of God is, that which is good and acceptable and perfect" (Rom 12:1–2). In a similar way he admonished the Corinthians, "Whether at home or absent, to be pleasing to [God]" (2 Cor 5:9; cf. Eph 5:10; Phil 4:18). He exhorted the believers at Thessalonica "to walk and please God (just as you actually do walk), that you may excel still more" (1 Thess 4:1).

After describing the spiritual characteristics and incapacities of those who are in the flesh, Paul again addresses those who **are not in the flesh but in the Spirit.** As Jesus explained to Nicodemus, "That which is born of the flesh is flesh, and that which is born of the Spirit is spirit" (John 3:6). Sinful human flesh can only reproduce more sinful human flesh. Only God's Holy Spirit can produce spiritual life.

A test of saving faith is the indwelling presence of the Holy Spirit. "You can be certain of your salvation," Paul is saying, **"if indeed the Spirit of God dwells in you."** *Oikeō* (**dwells**) has the idea of being in one's own home. In a marvelous and incomprehensible way, the very **Spirit of God** makes His home in the life of every person who trusts in Jesus Christ.

The opposite of that reality is also true: **But if anyone does not have the Spirit of Christ, he does not belong to Him.** The person who gives no evidence of the presence, power, and fruit of God's Spirit in his life has no legitimate claim to Christ as Savior and Lord. The person who demonstrates no desire for the things of God and has no inclination to avoid sin or passion to please God is not indwelt by the Holy Spirit and thus does not belong to Christ. In light of that sobering truth Paul admonishes those who claim to be Christians: "Test yourselves to see if you are in the faith; examine yourselves! Or do you not

THE TRIUMPH OF LOVE

recognize this about yourselves, that Jesus Christ is in you—unless indeed you fail the test?" (2 Cor 13:5).

And if Christ is in you, Paul continues to say to believers, **though the body is dead because of sin, yet the spirit is alive because of righteousness.** In other words, if God's Spirit indwells us, our own **spirit is alive because of righteousness,** that is, because of the divinely-imparted righteousness by which every believer is justified (Rom 3:21–26). In light of that perfect righteousness, all human attempts at being righteous are but rubbish (Phil 3:8).

Summing up what he has just declared in verses 5–10, Paul says, **But if the Spirit of Him who raised Jesus from the dead dwells in you, He who raised Christ Jesus from the dead will also give life to your mortal bodies through His Spirit who indwells you.** It was again the Holy Spirit who was the divine agent of Christ's resurrection. And just as the Spirit lifted Jesus out of physical death and gave Him life in His mortal body, so the Spirit, who dwells in the believer, gives to that believer new life now and forever (cf. John 6:63; 2 Cor 3:6).

THE HOLY SPIRIT EMPOWERS US FOR VICTORY OVER THE FLESH

So then, brethren, we are under obligation, not to the flesh, to live according to the flesh—for if you are living according to the flesh, you must die; but

if by the Spirit you are putting to death the deeds of the body, you will live. (8:12–13)

In his often-republished book *The Reformed Pastor*, the seventeenth century Puritan Richard Baxter wrote,

Take heed to yourselves, lest you live in those sins which you preach against in others, and lest you be guilty of that which daily you condemn. Will you make it your work to magnify God, and, when you have done, dishonour him as much as others? Will you proclaim Christ's governing power, and yet condemn it, and rebel yourselves? Will you preach his laws, and willfully break them? If sin be evil, why do you live in it? If it be not, why do you dissuade men from it? If it be dangerous, how dare you venture on it? If it be not, why do you tell men so? If God's threatenings be true, why do you not fear them? If they be false, why do you needlessly trouble men with them, and put them into such frights without a cause? Do you "know the judgment of God, that they who commit such things are worthy of death;" and yet will you do them? "Thou that teachest another, teachest thou not thyself? Thou that sayest a man should not commit adultery," or be drunk, or covetous, art thou such thyself? "Thou that makest thy boast of the law, through breaking the law dishonourest thou God?" What! Shall the same tongue speak evil that speakest against evil? Shall those lips censure, and slander, and backbite your neighbour, that cry down these and the like things in others? Take heed to yourselves, lest you cry down sin, and yet do not overcome it; lest, while you seek to bring it down in others, you bow to it, and become its slaves yourselves: "For of whom a man is overcome, of the same is he brought into bondage." "To whom ye yield yourselves servants to obey, his servants ye are to whom ye obey, whether of sin unto death, or of obedience unto righteousness." O brethren! It is easier to chide at sin, than to overcome it.... Many a tailor goes in rags, that maketh costly clothes for others; and many a cook scarcely licks his fingers, when he hath dressed for others the most costly dishes. ([Carlisle, PA: Banner of Truth, 1974], pp. 67–68)

Paul has just made clear (vv. 5–11) that every genuine Christian is indwelt by God's own Spirit and that his new spiritual life therefore will not be characterized by worldly, fleshly concerns and activities but by the things of God. The apostle's emphasis then turns, in verses 12–13, to the believer's responsibility to eliminate sin in his life through the indwelling Spirit.

By the phrase **so then,** Paul reminds his readers of the magnificent privileges of victory over sin that Christians have through the resident Holy Spirit. In the previous eleven verses of chapter 8, he has pointed out, among other things, that believers are no longer under God's condemnation, that they are set free from the law of sin and death, that they are no longer under the domination of sin, that they walk by the Spirit, that they have minds that are set on the Spirit, and that they have life and peace through the Spirit.

All biblical exhortations to believers are based on the blessings and promises they already have from the Lord. Without the provisions we have from Him, we would be unable to fulfill the commands we receive from Him. The children of Israel, for instance, were not commanded to take possession of the Promised Land until it was promised to them by God and they were prepared by Him to conquer it. In this letter to Rome, Paul's primary exhortations begin with chapter 12, after he has given countless reminders to his readers of their great spiritual privileges. In Ephesians he first gives three chapters that are largely a listing of spiritual benefits. Just before his beautiful doxology at the end of chapter 3, Paul prays that God "would grant you, according to the riches of His glory, to be strengthened with power through His Spirit in the inner man; so that Christ may dwell in your hearts through faith; and that you, being rooted and grounded in love, may be able to comprehend with all the saints what is the breadth and length and height and depth, and to know the love of Christ which surpasses knowledge, that you may be filled up to all the fullness of God" (Eph 3:16–19). Only then does he entreat fellow believers "to walk in a manner worthy of the calling with which you have been called" (4:1). Similar patterns are found in his letters to Galatia, Philippi, and Colossae, often noted by the word *therefore*.

Before the apostle gives the admonition in the present text, he refers affectionately to his readers as **brethren,** identifying them as fellow Christians, those to whom God promises victory over the flesh. He chooses a term of esteem and equality, not of superiority or paternalism, to refer to his brothers and sisters in Christ.

Paul then proceeds to set forth God's pattern for victory over the flesh. As God's children indwelt by His Spirit, we have no **obligation ... to the flesh, to live according to the flesh. The flesh** is the ugly complex of human sinful desires that includes the ungodly motives, affections, principles, purposes, words, and actions that sin generates through our bodies. **To live according to the flesh** is to be ruled and controlled by that evil complex. Because of Christ's saving work on our behalf, the sinful flesh no longer reigns over us, to debilitate us and drag us back into the pit of depravity into which we were all born. For that reason, **we are** no longer ruled by **the flesh** to **live** by its sinful ways.

Those who **are living according to the flesh ... must die.** The apostle is not warning genuine believers that they may lose their salvation and be condemned to death if they fall back into some of the ways of the flesh. He has already given the absolute assurance that "there is therefore now no condemnation for those who are in Christ Jesus" (8:1). He is rather saying that a person whose life is characterized by the things of **the flesh** is not a true Christian and is spiritually dead, no matter what his religious affiliations or activities may be. If he does not come to Christ in true faith, he **must die** the second death under God's final judgment.

Paul next restates the reason genuine Christians are no longer obligated to and bound by sin and are no longer under its condemnation. Although there will always be some lingering influence of **the flesh** until we meet the Lord, we have no excuse for sin to continue to corrupt our lives. The Christian's obligation is no longer to the flesh but to the **Spirit.** We have the resources of the **Spirit** of Christ within us to resist and put **to death the deeds of the body,** which result from **living according to the flesh.**

Putting **to death the deeds of the body** is a characteristic of God's children. The Scottish theologian David Brown wrote, "If you don't kill sin, sin will kill you." Jesus said, "If your right eye makes you stumble, tear it out, and throw it from you; for it is better for you that one of the parts of your body perish, than for your whole body to be thrown into hell. And if your right hand makes you stumble, cut it off, and throw it from you; for it is better for you that one of the parts of your body perish, than for your whole body to go into hell" (Matt 5:29–30). No action is too drastic in dealing with sin; no price is too great to pay in turning from sin to trust Jesus Christ and thereby escaping the damnation of eternal death in hell.

Paul here gives one of the many self-examination passages in Scripture. As noted above, the person who gives no evidence of the presence, power, and fruit of God's Spirit in his life has no legitimate claim to Christ as Savior and Lord. The obvious other side of that truth is that the person whose life is characterized by the sinful ways of the flesh is still in the flesh and is not in Christ. When Paul declares that believers are God's "workmanship, created in Christ Jesus for good works, which God prepared beforehand, that we should walk in them" (Eph 2:10), he is stating a fact, not a wish.

Like many of the members of the church in Corinth, an immature and disobedient Christian will inevitably lapse into some of the ways of the flesh (see 1 Cor 3:1). After he had been an apostle for many years, Paul himself confessed that even he was not yet spiritually flawless. "Not that I have already obtained it, or have already become perfect," he told the Philippians, "but I press on in order that I may lay hold of that for which also I was laid hold of by Christ Jesus. Brethren, I do not regard myself as having laid hold of it yet; but one thing I do: forgetting what lies behind and reaching forward to what lies ahead, I press on toward the goal for the prize of the upward call of God in Christ Jesus" (Phil 3:12–14). Paul had not yet achieved perfect righteousness in Christ, although that was the supreme objective of his life. Although his flesh sometimes held him back and temporarily interrupted the full joy of his fellowship with Christ, his basic heart's desire was to obey and please his Lord.

If a professing Christian habitually lives in sin and shows no concern for repentance, forgiveness, worship, or fellowship with other believers, he proves that he claims the name of Christ in vain. Many false Christians in the church work hard at keeping their lives pure in appearance, because other people think more highly of them for it and because they feel prouder of themselves when they act morally and benevolently than when they do not. But feeling better about oneself, the popular psychological cure-all for many people in our times, is the very heart of the proud sinful flesh, man's unredeemed selfishness and godless humanness. Doing good for one's own sake rather than for God's is not doing good at all, but is merely a hypocritical projection of the sin of self-love.

It should not be surprising that, as the world more and more advocates self-love and self-fulfillment, the problems of sexual promiscuity, abuse, and perversion, of stealing, lying, murder, suicide, hopelessness, and all other forms of moral and social ills are multiplying exponentially.

The pattern of a true believer's life, on the other hand, will show that he not only professes Christ but that he lives his life **by** Christ's **Spirit** and is habitually **putting to death the** sinful and ungodly **deeds of the body.** Consequently, he **will live,** that is, possess and persevere to the fulness of eternal life given him in Christ.

When God ordered King Saul to destroy *all* of the Amalekites and their livestock, Saul did not completely obey, sparing king Agag and keeping the best of the animals. When the prophet Samuel confronted Saul, the king tried to defend his actions by claiming his people insisted on keeping some of the flocks and that those animals would be sacrificed to God. Samuel rebuked the king, saying, "Has the Lord as much delight in burnt offerings and sacrifices as in obeying the voice of the Lord? Behold, to obey is better than sacrifice, and to heed than the fat of rams" (1 Sam 15:22). Despite the king's pleas for mercy, Samuel then proclaimed, "The Lord has torn the kingdom of Israel from you today, and has given it to your neighbor [David] who is better than you" (v. 28). Saul's failure to fully obey God cost him his throne.

God's people invariably fall back into sin when their focus turns away from the Almighty to themselves and to the things of the world. For that reason Paul admonished the believers at Colossae, "If then you have been raised up with Christ, keep seeking the things above, where Christ is, seated at the right hand of God. Set your mind on the things above, not on the things that are on earth. For you have died and your life is hidden with Christ in God" (Col 3:1–3). He then gave a partial but representative list of sins that Christians should kill by considering themselves dead to: "immorality, impurity, passion, evil desire, and greed, which amounts to idolatry. For it is on account of these things that the wrath of God will come, and in them you also once walked, when you were living in them. But now you also, put them all aside: anger, wrath, malice, slander, and abusive speech from your mouth. Do not lie to one another, since you laid aside the old self with its evil practices, and have put on the new self who is being renewed to a true knowledge according to the image of the One who created him" (vv. 5–10).

Paul is not suggesting the "Let go and let God" philosophy that is promoted by groups and leaders who advocate a so-called deeper life, in which one progressively rises to higher and higher levels of spirituality until sin and even temptation are virtually absent. That is not the kind of spiritual life Paul promises or that he personally experienced, as he testifies so movingly in Romans 7. As long as a believer is in his earthly body, he will be subject to the perils of the flesh and will need to keep putting its sins to death. Only in heaven will his need for practical sanctification end. Until then, all believers are admonished to put sin to death and to live in and for their new Sovereign, the Lord Jesus Christ (cf. Rom 6:3–11).

The Puritan John Owen warned that sin is never less quiet than when it seems to be most quiet, and its waters are for the most part deep when they are still (cf. *Sin and Temptation* [Portland, OR: Multnomah, 1983], p. xxi). Satan is likely to attack when a believer is most satisfied with his spiritual life. That is when pride, the chief of sins, easily sneaks into our lives unnoticed and leads us to believe that contentment with ourselves is contentment in God.

Scripture offers believers many helps for avoiding and killing sin in their lives. First, it is imperative to recognize the presence of sin in our flesh. We must be willing to confess honestly with Paul, "I find then the principle that evil is present in me, the one who wishes to do good" (Rom 7:21). If we do not admit to sin, we delude ourselves and become still more susceptible to its influence. Sin can become a powerful and destructive force in a believer's life if it is not recognized and put to death. Our remaining humanness is constantly ready to drag us back into the sinful ways of our life before Christ. Knowing that truth well, Peter admonishes, "Beloved, I urge you as aliens and strangers to abstain from fleshly lusts, which wage war against the soul" (1 Pet 2:11). If Christians did not live in constant danger from sin, such advice would be pointless.

Because of the influence of our human weaknesses and limitations on our thinking, it is often difficult to recognize sin in our lives. It can easily become camouflaged, often under the guise of something that seems trivial or insignificant, even righteous and good. We must therefore pray with David, "Search me, O God, and know my heart; try me and know my anxious thoughts; and see if there be any hurtful way in me, and lead me in the everlasting way" (Ps 139:23–24).

Haggai's counsel to ancient Israel is helpful for believers in any age: "Consider your ways!" (Hag 1:5, 7).

A second way for believers to kill sin in their lives is to have a heart fixed on God. David said to the Lord, "My heart is steadfast, O God, my heart is steadfast; I will sing, yes, I will sing praises!" (Ps 57:7). Another psalmist testified, "O that my ways may be established to keep Thy statutes! Then I shall not be ashamed when I look upon all Thy commandments" (Ps 119:5–6). In other words, when we know and obey God's Word, we are building up both our defenses and offenses against sin.

A third way for believers to kill sin in their lives is to meditate on God's Word. Many of the Lord's truths become clear only when we patiently immerse ourselves in a passage of Scripture and give the Lord opportunity to give us deeper understanding. David gives us the example with these words: "Thy word I have treasured in my heart, that I may not sin against Thee" (Ps 119:11).

A fourth way to destroy sin in our lives is to commune regularly with God in prayer. Peter calls us to "be of sound judgment and sober spirit for the purpose of prayer" (1 Pet 4:7). When we are faithful in these disciplines we discover how interrelated they are. It is often difficult to tell where study of God's word ends and meditation on it begins, and where meditation ends and prayer begins.

It should be emphasized that true prayer must always have an element of confession. Although we have the assurance that we belong to God and are free from condemnation, we also know that we can never come before Him completely sinless. "If we say that we have no sin, we are deceiving ourselves, and the truth is not in us," John warns believers. But "if we confess our sins, He is faithful and righteous to forgive us our sins and to cleanse us from all unrighteousness. If we say that we have not sinned, we make Him a liar, and His word is not in us" (1 John 1:8–10). The writer of Hebrews admonishes, "Let us therefore draw near with confidence to the throne of grace, that we may receive mercy and may find grace to help in time of need" (Heb 4:16). We need to be cleansed every time we come to Him.

Sincere prayer has a way of unmasking sin's deceit. When God's children open their minds and hearts to their heavenly Father, He lovingly reveals sins that otherwise would go unnoticed.

A fifth way to put to death sin in our lives is to practice obedience to God. Doing His will and His will alone in all the small issues of life can be training in habits that will hold up in the severe times of temptations.

As Paul has already made plain by the testimony from his own life in chapter 7, putting sin to death is often difficult, slow, and frustrating. Satan is the great adversary of God's people and will make every effort to drag them down into sin. But as they conquer sin in their lives through the power of the indwelling Holy Spirit, they not only are brought nearer to their heavenly Father but attain ever-increasing assurance that they are indeed His children and are eternally secure in Him.

When the New Testament speaks of such things as growing in grace, perfecting holiness, and renewing the inner man, it is referring to putting sin to death. Sin produced by the remaining flesh in which believers remain temporarily bound is all that stands between them and perfect godliness.

But Paul assures Christians that they have power for victory over the sinful flesh that still clings to them in this life. Apart from the Spirit's supernatural power, we could never succeed in putting to death the recurring sin in our lives. If we were left to our own resources, the struggle with sin would simply be flesh trying to overcome flesh, humanness trying to conquer humanness. Even as a Christian, Paul lamented, "For I know that nothing good dwells in me, that is, in my flesh; for the wishing is present in me, but the doing of the good is not" (Rom 7:18). Without the Holy Spirit, a Christian would have no more power to resist and defeat sin than does an unbeliever.

The Holy Spirit is virtually synonymous with divine power. Just before His ascension, Jesus promised the apostles, "You shall receive power when the Holy Spirit has come upon you; and you shall be My witnesses both in Jerusalem, and in all Judea and Samaria, and even to the remotest part of the earth" (Acts 1:8). Later in his account of the early church, Luke reports: "You know of Jesus of Nazareth, how God anointed Him with the Holy Spirit and with power, and how He went about doing good, and healing all who were oppressed by the devil; for God was with Him" (Acts 10:38). In his gospel, Luke relates the angel's announcement to Mary concerning the divine conception and birth of Jesus: "The Holy Spirit will come upon you, and the power of the Most High will overshadow you; and for that reason the holy offspring shall be called the Son of God" (Luke 1:35).

The prophet Micah wrote, "I am filled with power—with the Spirit of the Lord—and with justice and courage to make known to Jacob his rebellious act, even to Israel his sin" (Mic 3:8). Concerning the rebuilding of the Temple, an angel encouraged Zerubbabel through the prophet Zechariah: "This is the word of the Lord to Zerubbabel saying, 'Not by might nor by power, but by My Spirit,' says the Lord of hosts" (Zech 4:6). In other words, the Spirit's divine power would undergird Zerubbabel and would far surpass the power of the wicked men who sought to thwart his work.

Paul reports later in this epistle that the salvation of many Gentiles through his ministry was accomplished only "in the power of the Spirit" (Rom 15:19), and he prayed that believers in the Ephesian church would "be strengthened with power through His Spirit in the inner man" (Eph 3:16).

Paul's main point in Romans 8:13 is that, by the power of **the Spirit** who **dwells in** them, Christians are able successfully to resist and destroy sin in their lives. "The weapons of our warfare are not of the flesh," Paul reminds us, "but divinely powerful for the destruction of fortresses" (2 Cor 10:4). It is such confidence in the power of the Holy Spirit that gives hope to the frustration Paul expressed in Romans 7:24–25, a frustration that every Christian faces from time to time.

Speaking of the believer's conflict with sin, Paul told the Galatians that "the flesh sets its desire against the Spirit, and the Spirit against the flesh; for these are in opposition to one another, so that you may not do the things that you please" (Gal 5:17). A few verses later he declares that "those who belong to Christ Jesus have crucified the flesh with its passions and desires. If we live by the Spirit, let us also walk by the Spirit" (vv. 24–25). In other words, because our inner, spiritual lives are indwelt by the Holy Spirit, our behavior should be according to His will and in His power. Through the Holy Spirit who indwells him, every true Christian has the divine resource to have victory over Satan, over the world, and over sin.

In his letter to Ephesus, Paul refers to the believer's continual need to rely on the Spirit's power, and he admonishes: "Do not get drunk with wine, for that is dissipation, but be filled with the Spirit" (Eph 5:18). A more literal translation is, "keep being filled with the Spirit." The idea is, "Always rely on the power of the Holy Spirit, who resides within you and is always available to strengthen and protect you." To be filled with the Spirit is to have one's mind completely under His divine control. This requires the Word's dwelling richly in the believer (cf. Col 3:16). And when our minds are under God's control, our behavior inevitably will be as well. It is not a matter of available power but of available will. By the Spirit's power, all believers are able "to walk in a manner worthy of the calling with which [they] have been called" (Eph 4:1). Those who truly "put on the Lord Jesus Christ" will "make no provision for the flesh in regard to its lusts" (Rom 13:14).

Being controlled by God's Spirit comes from being obedient to His Word. The Spirit-filled life does not come through mystical or ecstatic experiences but from studying and submitting oneself to Scripture. As a believer faithfully and submissively saturates his mind and heart with God's truth, his Spirit-controlled behavior will follow as surely as night follows day. When we are filled with God's truth and led by His Spirit, even our involuntary reactions—those that happen when we don't have time to consciously decide what to do or say—will be godly.

03

LIFE IN THE SPIRIT—PART 3
THE SPIRIT CONFIRMS
OUR ADOPTION

ROMANS 8:14–16

F or all who are being led by the Spirit of God, these are sons of God. For you have not received a spirit of slavery leading to fear again, but you have received a spirit of adoption as sons by which we cry out, "Abba! Father!" The Spirit Himself bears witness with our spirit that we are children of God ... (8:14–16)

This is one of the richest and most beautiful passages in all of Scripture. Using the figure of adoption, Paul explains the believer's intimate and permanent relationship to God as a beloved child.

In these verses, Paul continues to disclose the ways in which God confirms that believers are eternally related to Him as His children, testifying that we are led, given access to God, and granted inner assurance by His own Spirit. These three means of assurance are closely related and intertwined, but each presents a distinctive truth about the Spirit's work in the believer's life.

WE ARE LED BY THE SPIRIT

For all who are being led by the Spirit of God, these are sons of God. (8:14)

The first inner confirmation of adoption is the believer's **being led by the Spirit of God.** A person who is truly experiencing the leading hand of God at work in his life can be certain he is God's child.

It is important to note the tense Paul uses here. **Are being led** translates the present passive indicative of *agō*, indicating that which already exists. The phrase **are being led** does not, however, indicate uninterrupted leading by **the Spirit.** Otherwise the many New Testament admonitions and warnings to Christians would be meaningless. But the genuine believer's life is basically characterized by the Spirit's leading, just as it is basically characterized by Christ's righteousness.

A merely professing Christian does not and cannot be **led by the Spirit of God.** He may be moral, conscientious, generous, active in his church and other Christian organizations, and exhibit many other commendable traits. But the only accomplishments, religious or otherwise, he can make claim to are those of his own doing. His life may be outstandingly religious, but because he lives it in the power of the flesh, he can never be truly spiritual and he will never have the inner conviction of God's leading and empowering.

When someone confides in me that he has doubts about his salvation, I often respond by asking if he ever senses God's leading in his life. If he answers yes, I remind him of Paul's assurance in this verse: **All who are being led by the Spirit of God, these are sons of God.**

God's children are secure in Him even when they are not as responsive and obedient to His leading as they ought to be. But that is not to say that a child of God will always feel secure. The Christian who neglects study of Scripture, who neglects God in prayer, who neglects fellowship with God's people, and who is careless about his obedience to God will invariably have doubts about his salvation, because he is indifferent to God and the things of God. Even for the obedient child of God, doubts about his relationship to God can easily slip into the mind during times of pain, sorrow, failure, or disappointment. Satan, the great accuser of God's people, is always ready to take advantage of such circumstances to plant seeds of uncertainty.

But our heavenly Father wants His children to be certain at all times that they belong to Him and are secure in Him. As Paul has just stated (Rom 8:13), a person who is succeeding in putting to death sin in his life is not doing so in his own power, that is, in the power of the flesh, but by the power of the Spirit. Those who see victory over sin in their lives, who see their sinful desires and practices diminishing, can be certain they **are sons of God,** because only God's **Spirit** can bring victory over sin. In the same way—when we begin to understand biblical truths that have long puzzled us, when we experience God's convicting our consciences, when we grieve for the Lord's sake when we sin—we have the divine assurance that we **are sons of God,** because only the indwelling **Spirit of God** can instill such understanding, conviction, and godly sorrow.

Our finite minds cannot comprehend how the Spirit leads a believer, just as we cannot fully understand any of the supernatural work of God. We do, however, know that our heavenly Father does not force His will on His children. He seeks our willing obedience, which, by definition, cannot be coerced. It is when we are genuinely submissive to Him that our Lord supernaturally reshapes and redirects our will into voluntary conformity with His own.

God saves men through their faith in Him, and He leads those he saves through the same human channel of faith. "Trust in the Lord with all your heart, and do not lean on your own understanding," the writer of Proverbs counsels. "In all your ways acknowledge Him, and He will make your paths straight" (Prov 3:5–6). The seeking, willing, and obedient heart is open to the Lord's leading. David prayed, "Make me know Thy ways, O Lord; teach me Thy paths. Lead me in Thy truth and teach me, for Thou art the God of my salvation; for Thee I wait all the day" (Ps 25:4–5). Later in that psalm he reminds us that God "leads the humble in justice, and He teaches the humble His way" (Ps 25:9). In another psalm he entreated the Lord, "Teach me to do Thy will, for Thou art my God; let Thy good Spirit lead me on level ground" (Ps 143:10).

Isaiah assures us that if we truly seek the Lord's will. He is already standing beside us, as it were, ready to say, "This is the way, walk in it" (Isa 30:21). The prophet was not speaking necessarily of an audible voice, but the voice of the believer's God-directed conscience, a conscience instructed by God's Word and attuned to His Spirit. Isaiah also assures us that the Lord is continually ready and eager to lead His people in the right way. Prophesying in the name of the preincarnate Christ, the prophet declared, "Come near to Me, listen to this: from the first I have not spoken in secret, from the time it took place, I was there. And now the Lord God has sent Me, and His Spirit. Thus says the Lord, your Redeemer, the Holy One of Israel; 'I am the Lord your God, who teaches you to profit, who leads you in the way you should go'" (Isa 48:16–17). Jeremiah acknowledged, "I know, O Lord, that a man's way is not in himself; nor is it in a man who walks to direct his steps" (Jer 10:23). Even the child of God cannot discern divine truth by his own intelligence or obey it in his own power.

God's Spirit sovereignly leads His children in many ways, sometimes in ways that are direct and unique. But the primary ways by which He promises to lead us are those of illumination and sanctification.

In the first way, God leads His children by illumination, by divinely clarifying His Word to make it understandable to our finite and still sin-tainted minds. As we read, meditate on, and pray over Scripture, the indwelling Spirit of God becomes our divine interpreter. This begins with the conviction of sin that leads through saving belief into the whole of the Christian life.

Although Joseph was not indwelt by the Holy Spirit as are believers under the New Covenant, even the pagan Egyptian ruler recognized him as a man "in whom is a divine spirit." Consequently, "Pharaoh said to Joseph, 'Since God has informed you of all this, there is no one so discerning and wise as you are'" (Gen 41:38–39).

The Old Testament saint who wrote Psalm 119, which so eloquently glorifies God's Word, knew he needed the Lord's divine help both to understand and to obey that Word. Every believer should continually pray with the psalmist: "Make me walk in the path of Thy commandments, for I delight in it" (Ps 119:35), and, "Establish my footsteps in Thy word, and do not let any iniquity have dominion over me" (Ps 119:133).

During the Upper Room Discourse, shortly before His betrayal and arrest, Jesus told the apostles, "These things I have spoken to you, while abiding with you. But the Helper, the Holy Spirit, whom the Father will send in My name, He will teach you all things, and bring to your remembrance all that I said to you" (John 14:25–26). That promise had special significance for the apostles, who would become Christ's uniquely authoritative witnesses to His truth after His ascension back to heaven. But the promise also applies in a general way to all believers after Pentecost. From that time on, *every* believer has been indwelt by Christ's own Holy Spirit, whose ministry to us includes that of shedding divine light on scriptural truths that otherwise are beyond our comprehension.

During one of His postresurrection appearances, Jesus said to the eleven remaining apostles, "'These are My words which I spoke to you while I was still with you, that all things which are written about Me in the Law of Moses and the Prophets and the Psalms must be fulfilled.' Then He opened their minds to understand the Scriptures" (Luke 24:44–45). Again Jesus' words had unique significance for the apostles, but in a similar way the Lord opens the minds of *all* His disciples "to understand the Scriptures."

On behalf of the Ephesian believers Paul prayed that "the God of our Lord Jesus Christ, the Father of glory, may give to you a spirit of wisdom and of revelation in the knowledge of Him. I pray that the eyes of your heart may be enlightened, so that you may know what is the hope of His calling, what are the riches of the glory of His inheritance in the saints, and what is the surpassing greatness of His power toward us who believe. These are in accordance with the working of the strength of His might" (Eph 1:17–19). Later in that epistle Paul offered a similar prayer, asking that God "would grant you, according to the riches of His glory, to be strengthened with power through His Spirit in the inner man; so that Christ may dwell in your hearts through faith; and that you, being rooted and grounded in love, may be able to comprehend with all the saints what is the breadth and length and height and depth, and to know the love of Christ which surpasses knowledge, that you may be filled up to all the fulness of God" (3:16–19).

Paul assured the saints at Colossae that "we have not ceased to pray for you and to ask that you may be filled with the knowledge of His will in all spiritual wisdom and understanding" (Col 1:9). His devotion to them was again expressed in the loving words: "Let the word of Christ richly dwell within you, with all wisdom teaching and admonishing one another with psalms and hymns and spiritual songs, singing with thankfulness in your hearts to God" (3:16).

Perhaps the most definitive passage on the illuminating work of the Holy Spirit is in Paul's first letter to Corinth. "A natural man does not accept the things of the Spirit of God," he asserts; "for they are foolishness to him, and he cannot understand them, because they are spiritually appraised. But he who is spiritual appraises all things, yet he himself is appraised by no man. For who has known the mind of the Lord, that he should instruct Him? But we have the mind of Christ" (1 Cor 2:14–16). In other words, even God's own children could not understand their heavenly Father's Word apart from the illuminating work of His Spirit within them.

The second major way in which **the Spirit** leads God's children is by their sanctification. **The Spirit** not only illuminates our minds to understand Scripture but divinely assists us in obeying it, and that obedience becomes another testimony to our salvation. The humble child of God knows he cannot please his Lord in his own power. But he also knows that, when he sincerely labors in the Lord's work in accordance with the commands and principles of Scripture, the Holy Spirit will bless that work in ways far beyond what the believer's own abilities could have produced. It is then that our heavenly Father is deeply pleased with us, not for what we have accomplished but for what we have allowed Him to accomplish in and through us. It is not our work in itself but our spirit of obedience to Him and dependence on Him as we do His work that brings joy to our heavenly Father's heart. It is through our faithful obedience that we experience the gracious working of **the Spirit** in our lives. And, as with His divine illumination, His divine work of sanctification gives us assurance that we are indeed **sons of God.**

"I say, walk by the Spirit, and you will not carry out the desire of the flesh," Paul admonished the Galatians. "For the flesh sets its desire against the Spirit, and the Spirit against the flesh; for these are in opposition to one another, so that you may not do the things that you please" (Gal 5:16–17). And because "we live by the Spirit," he goes on to say, "let us also walk by the Spirit" (v. 25).

As with illumination and all other divine works, we cannot understand exactly *how* God accomplishes His sanctifying work in us. We simply know from His Word, and often from experience, that He performs spiritual works in and through us that are not produced by our own efforts or power. Often we become aware of the Spirit's activity only in retrospect, as we see His sanctifying power bearing fruit in our lives from seeds planted long beforehand. We also have the blessed assurance that, although we are not consciously aware of the Spirit's work in us at all times, He is nevertheless *performing* His divine work in us at all times. He not only gives and sustains our spiritual life, He is our spiritual life.

It is our heavenly Father's great desire for His children to submit to the leading of His Spirit, for the sake of His glory and for the sake of their spiritual fruitfulness, well-being, and peace.

WE ARE GIVEN ACCESS TO GOD BY THE SPIRIT

For you have not received a spirit of slavery leading to fear again, but you have received a spirit of adoption as sons by which we cry out, "Abba! Father!" (8:15)

A second way in which the Holy Spirit confirms our adoption as God's children is by freeing us from the **spirit of slavery** that inevitably leads us **to fear again.** Because God's "children share in flesh and blood," we are told by the writer of Hebrews, "He Himself [Christ] likewise also partook of the same, that through death

He might render powerless him who had the power of death, that is, the devil; and might deliver those who through fear of death were subject to slavery all their lives" (Heb 2:14–15).

No matter how cleverly they may manage to mask or deny the reality of it, sinful men are continually subject to fear because they continually live in sin and are therefore continually under God's judgment. Slavery to sin brings slavery to fear, and one of the gracious works of the Holy Spirit is to deliver God's children from both.

John Donne, the seventeenth-century English poet who later became pastor and dean of St. Paul's Cathedral in London, wrote in "A Hymn to God the Father" the following touching lines:

> Wilt Thou forgive that sin where I begun,
> Which was my sin, though it were done before?
> Wilt Thou forgive that sin, through which I run,
> And do run still, though still I do deplore?
> When Thou hast done, Thou hast not done;
> For I have more....
> I have a sin of fear, that when I have spun
> My last thread, I shall perish on the shore;
> But swear by Thy self that at my death Thy Son
> Shall shine as he shines now and heretofore:
> And, having done that, Thou hast done,
> I fear no more.

Paul reminded Timothy that our heavenly Father "has not given us a spirit of timidity [or, fear], but of power and love and discipline" (2 Tim 1:7). John assures us that "there is no fear in love; but perfect love casts out fear, because fear involves punishment, and the one who fears is not perfected in love" (1 John 4:18).

At this point in Romans, Paul is not so much emphasizing the transaction of **adoption** as the believer's assurance of it. Through the regenerating work of the Holy Spirit, we not only are truly and permanently adopted as children of God but are given **a spirit of adoption.** That is, God makes certain His children *know* they are His children. Because of His Spirit dwelling in our hearts, our **spirit** recognizes that we are always privileged to come before God as our beloved Father.

The term **adoption** is filled with the ideas of love, grace, compassion, and intimate relationship. It is the action by which a husband and wife decide to take a boy or girl who is not their physical offspring into their family as their own child. When that action is taken by the proper legal means, the adopted child attains all the rights and privileges of a member of the family.

The first adoption recorded in Scripture was that of Moses. When Pharaoh ordered all the male Hebrew children slain, Moses' mother placed him in a waterproof basket and set him in the Nile River among some reeds. When Pharaoh's daughter came to the river with her maids to bathe, she saw the basket and had one of her maids retrieve it. She immediately realized the infant was Hebrew but took pity on him. Moses' sister, Miriam, had been watching nearby and she offered to find a nursemaid for the child, as her mother had instructed. With the approval of Pharaoh's daughter, Miriam brought her own mother, who was then paid to take Moses home and nurse him. When Moses was a young boy, he was brought to the palace and adopted by Pharaoh's daughter (see Exod 2:1–10).

Because Esther's parents had died, she was adopted by an older cousin named Mordecai, who loved her as a father and took special care to look after her welfare (see Esth 2:5–11).

Perhaps the most touching adoption mentioned in the Old Testament was that of Mephibosheth, the crippled son of Jonathan and the sole remaining descendent of Saul. When King David learned about Mephibosheth, he gave him all the land that had belonged to his grandfather Saul and honored this son of his dearest friend, Jonathan, by having him dine regularly at the king's table in the palace at Jerusalem (see 2 Sam 9:1–13).

Pharaoh's daughter adopted Moses out of pity and sympathy. And although Mordecai dearly loved Esther, his adoption of her was also prompted by family duty. But David's adoption of Mephibosheth was motivated purely by gracious love. In many ways, David's adoption of Mephibosheth pictures God's adoption of believers. David took the initiative in seeking out Mephibosheth and bringing him to the palace. And although Mephibosheth was the son of David's closest friend, he was also the grandson and sole heir of Saul, who had sought repeatedly to kill David. Being crippled in both feet, Mephibosheth was helpless to render David any significant service; he could only accept his sovereign's bounty. The very name Mephibosheth means "a shameful thing," and he had lived for a number of years in Lo-debar, which means "the barren land" (lit., "no pasture"). David brought this outcast to dine at his table as his own son and graciously granted him a magnificent inheritance to which he was no longer legally entitled.

That is a beautiful picture of the spiritual adoption whereby God graciously and lovingly seeks out unworthy men and women on His own initiative and makes them His children, solely on the basis of their trust in His true Son, Jesus Christ. Because of their adoption, believers will share the full inheritance of the Son. To all Christians God declares, "'I will welcome you, and I will be a father to you, and you shall be sons and daughters to Me,' says the Lord Almighty" (2 Cor 6:17–18). Paul gives us the unspeakably marvelous assurance that God has "predestined us to adoption as sons through Jesus Christ to Himself, according to the kind intention of His will" (Eph 1:5).

For some people today, the concept of adoption carries the idea of second-class status in the family. In the Roman culture of Paul's day, however, an adopted child, especially an adopted son, sometimes had greater prestige and privilege than the natural children. According to Roman law, a father's rule over his children was absolute. If he was disappointed in his natural sons' skill, character, or any other attribute, he would search diligently for a boy available for adoption who demonstrated the qualities he desired. If the boy proved himself worthy, the father would take the necessary legal steps for adoption. At the death of the father, a favored adopted son would sometimes inherit the father's title, the major part of the estate, and would be the primary progenitor of the family name. Because of its obvious great importance, the process of Roman adoption involved several carefully prescribed legal procedures. The first step totally severed the boy's legal and social relationship to his natural family, and the second step placed him permanently into his new family. In addition to that, all of his previous debts and other obligations were eradicated, as if they had never existed. For the transaction to become legally binding, it also required the presence of seven reputable witnesses, who could testify, if necessary, to any challenge of the adoption after the father's death.

Paul doubtless was well aware of that custom, and may have had it in mind as he penned this section of

Romans. He assures believers of the wondrous truth that they are indeed God's adopted children, and that because of that immeasurably gracious relationship they have the full right and privilege to **cry out, "Abba!"** to God as their heavenly **Father,** just as every child does to his earthly father. The fact that believers have the compelling desire to cry out in intimate petition and praise to their loving Father, along with their longing for fellowship and communion with God, is evidence of the indwelling Holy Spirit, which indwelling proves one's salvation and gives assurance of eternal life.

Abba is an informal Aramaic term for **Father,** connoting intimacy, tenderness, dependence, and complete lack of fear or anxiety. Modern English equivalents would be Daddy, or Papa. When Jesus was agonizing in the Garden of Gethsemane as He was about to take upon Himself the sins of the world, He used that name of endearment, praying, "Abba! Father! All things are possible for Thee; remove this cup from Me; yet not what I will, but what Thou wilt" (Mark 14:36).

When we are saved, our old sinful life is completely cancelled in God's eyes, and we have no more reason to fear sin or death, because Christ has conquered those two great enemies on our behalf. In Him we are given a new divine nature and become a true child, with all the attendant blessings, privileges, and inheritance.

And until we see our Lord face-to-face, His own Holy Spirit will be a ceaseless witness to the authenticity of our adoption into the family of God.

The idea of Christians being God's adopted children was clearly understood by Paul's contemporaries to signify great honor and privilege. In his letter to Ephesus, the apostle exults, "Blessed be the God and Father of our Lord Jesus Christ, who has blessed us with every spiritual blessing in the heavenly places in Christ, just as He chose us in Him before the foundation of the world, that we should be holy and blameless before Him. In love He predestined us to adoption as sons through Jesus Christ to Himself, according to the kind intention of His will" (Eph 1:3–5). Countless ages ago, before He created the first human being in His divine image, God sovereignly chose every believer to be His beloved and eternal child!

It should be kept in mind that, marvelous as it is, the term **adoption** does not fully illustrate God's work of salvation. The believer is also cleansed from sin, saved from its penalty of death, spiritually reborn, justified, sanctified, and ultimately glorified. But those who are saved by their faith in Jesus Christ by the work of His grace have no higher title than that of adopted child of God. That name designates their qualification to share full inheritance with Christ. It is therefore far from incidental that Paul both introduces and closes this chapter with assurances to believers that they are no longer, and never again can be, under God's condemnation (see 8:1, 38–39).

WE ARE ASSURED BY THE SPIRIT

The Spirit Himself bears witness with our spirit that we are children of God ... (8:16)

To give us even further assurance of our eternal relationship to Him, the Lord's Holy **Spirit Himself bears witness with our spirit that we are children of God.** As noted above, just as the witnesses to a Roman adoption had the responsibility of testifying to its validity, so the indwelling Holy **Spirit Himself** is constantly present to provide inner testimony to our divine adoption. He certainly does that through the inner work of illumination and sanctification, as well as through the longing for communion with God.

But here Paul does not have in mind just some mystical small voice saying we are saved. Rather, he may be referring to the fruit of the Spirit (Gal 5:22–23), which, when the Spirit produces it, gives the believer assurance. Or, he may be thinking of the power for service (Acts 1:8), which when experienced is evidence of the Spirit's presence, thus assuring one of salvation.

When believers are compelled by love for God, feel deep hatred for sin, reject the world, long for Christ's return, love other Christians, experience answered prayer, discern between truth and error, long for and move toward Christlikeness, the work of the Holy Spirit is evidenced and those believers have witness that they truly **are children of God.**

The nineteenth-century British pastor Billy Bray seemed never to have lacked that inner testimony. He had been converted from a life of drunken debauchery while reading John Bunyan's *Visions of Heaven and Hell*. He was so continuously overjoyed by God's grace and goodness that he said, "I can't help praising the Lord. As I go along the street, I lift up one foot, and it seems to say, 'Glory.' And I lift up the other, and it seems to say, 'Amen.' And so they keep on like that all the time I am walking."

Whenever the world, other Christians, or we ourselves question that we are truly saved, we can appeal to the indwelling **Spirit** to settle the question in our hearts. Providing that assurance is one of His most precious ministries to us.

John offers the encouraging words, "Little children, let us not love with word or with tongue, but in deed and truth. We shall know by this that we are of the truth, and shall assure our heart before Him, in whatever our heart condemns us" (1 John 3:18–20*a*). That is objective evidence that we are truly God's children. John then reminds us of the subjective evidence our gracious Lord provides: "God is greater than our heart, and knows all things.

Beloved, if our heart does not condemn us, we have confidence before God" (vv. 20b–21).

04

THE HOLY SPIRIT GUARANTEES OUR GLORY—PART 1 THE INCOMPARABLE GAIN OF GLORY

ROMANS 8:17–18

Ａnd if children, heirs also, heirs of God and fellow heirs with Christ, if indeed we suffer with Him in order that we may also be glorified with Him.

For I consider that the sufferings of this present time are not worthy to be compared with the glory that is to be revealed to us. (8:17–18)

Whether consciously or not, every genuine Christian lives in the light and hope of glory. That hope is perhaps summed up best by John in his first epistle: "Beloved, now we are children of God, and it has not appeared as yet what we shall be. We know that, when He appears, we shall be like Him, because we shall see Him just as He is" (1 John 3:2). Because of our consummate trust in Jesus Christ as Lord and Savior, God graciously adopted us as His own children, and one day "we shall be like Him," like the perfect, sinless Son of God who took our sin upon Himself in order that we might share not only His righteousness but His glory!

In addition to freeing believers from sin and death (Rom 8:2–3), enabling them to fulfill God's law (v. 4), changing their nature (vv. 5–11), empowering them for victory (vv. 12–13), and confirming their adoption as God's children (vv. 14–16), the Holy Spirit guarantees their ultimate glory (vv. 17–30). In verses 17–18 Paul focuses on believers' incomparable spiritual gain through the divine glory that they are guaranteed.

The various aspects and stages of salvation of which the Bible speaks—such as regeneration, new birth, justification, sanctification, and glorification—can be distinguished but never separated. None of those can exist without the others. They are inextricably woven into the seamless fabric of God's sovereign work of redemption.

There can therefore be no loss of salvation between justification and glorification. Consequently, there can never be justification without glorification. "Whom [God] predestined, these He also called; and whom He called, these He also justified; and whom He justified, these He also glorified" (Rom 8:30). Justification is the beginning of salvation and glorification is its completion. Once it has begun, God *will not* stop it, and no other power in the universe is *able* to stop it. "Neither death, nor life, nor angels, nor principalities, nor things present, nor things to come, nor powers, nor height, nor depth, nor any other created thing, shall be able to separate us from the love of God, which is in Christ Jesus our Lord" (Rom 8:38–39). During His earthly ministry, Jesus declared unequivocally: "All that the Father gives Me shall come to Me, and the one who comes to Me I will certainly not cast out.... And this is the will of Him who sent Me, that of all that He has given Me I lose nothing, but raise it up on the last day. For this is the will of My Father, that everyone who beholds the Son and believes in Him, may have eternal life; and I Myself will raise him up on the last day" (John 6:37, 39–40).

Because he was created in the image of God, man was made with a glorious nature. Before the Fall, he was without sin and, in a way that Scripture does not reveal, he radiated the glory of his Creator. But when Adam fell by disobeying the single command of God, man lost not only his sinlessness and innocence but also his glory and its attendant dignity and honor. It is for that reason that all men now "fall short of the glory of God" (Rom 3:23).

Fallen men seem basically to know they are devoid of glory, and they often strive tirelessly to gain glory for themselves. The contemporary obsession with achieving self-esteem is a tragic reflection of man's sinful and futile efforts to regain glory apart from holiness.

The ultimate purpose of salvation is to forgive and to cleanse men of their sin and to restore to them God's glory and thereby bring to Him still greater glory through the working of that sovereign act of grace. The glory that believers are destined to receive through Jesus Christ, however, will far surpass the glory man had before the Fall, because perfection far exceeds innocence. Glorification marks the completion and perfection of salvation. Therefore, as the late British pastor and theologian Martyn Lloyd-Jones rightly observed in his exposition of our text, salvation cannot stop at any point short of entire perfection or it is not salvation. Pointing up that truth, Paul told the Philippian believers, "For I am confident of this very thing, that He who began a good work in you will perfect it until the day of Christ Jesus" (Phil 1:6).

Salvation brings continual growth in divine glory until it is perfected in the likeness of Jesus Christ Himself. "But we all, with unveiled face beholding as in a mirror the glory of the Lord, are being transformed into the same image from glory to glory, just as from the Lord, the Spirit" (2 Cor 3:18). As part of His ministry to us during our lives on earth, the Holy Spirit carries us from one level of glory to another.

In proclaiming the incomparable gain believers have in their divinely-bestowed glory, Paul focuses first on the heirs (8:17*a*), then on the source (v. 17*b*), the extent (v. 17*c*), the proof (v. 17*c*), and finally the comparison (v. 18).

THE HEIRS OF GLORY

And if children, heirs also … (8:17)

The emphasis in Romans 8:17–18 on believers' glory is closely related to their adoption as God's children (see vv. 14–16). As is clear from that preceding context, the **if** in verse 17 does not carry the idea of possibility or doubt but of reality and causality, and might be better translated "because." In other words, because *all* believers have the leading of the Holy Spirit (v. 14) and His witness (v. 16) that they are indeed **children** of God, they are thereby **heirs also.**

The heavenly angels not only serve God directly but also serve believers, because they are God's children and heirs. "Are they [angels] not all ministering spirits, sent out to render service for the sake of those who will inherit salvation?" the writer of Hebrews asks rhetorically (Heb 1:14). Because of our faith in His Son Jesus Christ, God the Father "has qualified us to share in the inheritance of the saints in light" (Col 1:12).

As explained in the last chapter, Paul's figure of adoption seems to correspond more to Roman law and custom than to Jewish. We might expect this, because Paul was writing to believers in Rome. And although many of them doubtless were Jewish, if their families had lived there for several generations, they would be as familiar with the Roman custom as the Jewish.

In Jewish tradition, the eldest son normally received a double portion of his father's inheritance. In Roman society, on the other hand, although a father had the prerogative of giving more to one child than to the others, normally all children received equal shares. And under Roman law, inherited possessions enjoyed more protection than those that were bought or worked for. Perhaps reflecting those Roman customs and laws, Paul's emphasis in this passage is on the equality of God's children and the security of their adoption.

Paul told the Galatians, "If you belong to Christ, then you are Abraham's offspring, heirs according to promise" (Gal 3:29; cf. 4:7). Here Paul is referring to spiritual heritage, citing Abraham, "the father of all who believe" (Rom 4:11), as the human archetype of the adopted child and heir of God.

THE SOURCE OF GLORY

heirs of God ... (8:17*b*)

The source of believers' incomparable glory is **God,** their heavenly Father, who has adopted them as His own children and **heirs.** Paul assured the Colossian Christians "that from the Lord you will receive the reward of the inheritance" (Col 3:24). This inheritance is only God's to give, and He sovereignly bestows it, without exception, on those who become His children and heirs through faith in His divine Son, Jesus Christ.

In His description of the sheep and goats judgment in the last days, Jesus reveals the astounding truth that our inheritance with Him was ordained by God in eternity past! "Then the King will say to those on His right, 'Come, you who are blessed of My Father, inherit the kingdom prepared for you from the foundation of the world'" (Matt 25:34). God does not adopt His children as an afterthought but according to His predetermined plan of redemption, which began before "the foundation of the world."

The value of an inheritance is determined by the worth of the one who bequeaths it, and the inheritance of Christians is from the Creator, Sustainer, and Owner of the world. **God** not only is the source of our inheritance but is Himself our inheritance. Of all the good things in the universe, the most precious is the Creator of the universe Himself. The psalmist declared, "Whom have I in heaven but Thee? And besides Thee, I desire nothing on earth" (Ps 73:25). Jeremiah wrote, "'The Lord is my portion,' says my soul, 'Therefore I have hope in Him'" (Lam 3:24). In his vision on the island of Patmos, John "heard a loud voice from the [heavenly] throne, saying, 'Behold, the tabernacle of God is among men, and He shall dwell among them, and they shall be His people, and God Himself shall be among them'" (Rev 21:3). The greatest blessing God's children will have in heaven will be the eternal presence of their God.

THE EXTENT OF GLORY

and fellow heirs with Christ ... (8:17*c*)

Many of us are heirs of those who have very little to bequeath in earthly possessions, and our human inheritance will amount to little, perhaps nothing. But just as God's resources are limitless, so our spiritual inheritance is limitless, because, as His **fellow heirs,** we share in everything that the true Son of God, Jesus **Christ,** inherits.

Paul exulted, "Blessed be the God and Father of our Lord Jesus Christ, who has blessed us with every spiritual blessing in the heavenly places in Christ, ... also we have obtained an inheritance, having been predestined according to His purpose who works all things after the counsel of His will" (Eph 1:3, 11). God the Father has appointed Jesus Christ the "heir of all things" (Heb 1:2), and because we are **fellow heirs** with Him, we are destined to receive all that He receives!

In the arithmetic of earth, if each heir receives an equal share of an inheritance, each gets only a certain fraction of the whole amount. But heaven is not under such limits, and *every* adopted child of God will receive the *full* inheritance with the Son. Everything that **Christ** receives by divine right, we will receive by divine grace. The parable of the laborers in Matthew 20:1–16 illustrates this graciousness, showing that all who serve Christ will receive the same eternal reward, irrespective of differences in their service.

Believers one day will enter into the eternal joy of their Master (Matt 25:21), who, for the sake of that joy, "endured the cross, despising the shame, and has sat down at the right hand of the throne of God" (Heb 12:2). Believers will sit on the heavenly throne with Christ and rule there with Him (Rev 3:21; cf. 20:4; Luke 22:30), bearing forever the very image of their Savior and Lord

(1 Cor 15:49; 1 John 3:2). In the infinite "grace of our Lord Jesus Christ, ... though He was rich, yet for [our] sake He became poor, that [we] through His poverty might become rich" (2 Cor 8:9). In His great high priestly prayer, Jesus spoke to His Father of the incredible and staggering truth that everyone who believes in Him will be one with Him and will share His full glory: "The glory which Thou hast given Me I have given to them; that they may be one, just as We are one" (John 17:22). We will not intrude on Christ's prerogatives, because, in His gracious will, He Himself bestows His glory on us and asks His Father to confirm that endowment.

It is not that believers will become gods, as some cults teach, but that we will receive, by our joint inheritance with Christ, all the blessings and grandeur that God has. We are "justified by His grace [in order that] we might be made heirs according to the hope of eternal life" (Titus 3:7). Jesus Christ "is the mediator of a new covenant, in order that since a death has taken place for the redemption of the transgressions that were committed under the first covenant, those who have been called may receive the promise of the eternal inheritance" (Heb 9:15).

The Christian who is not eagerly looking for Christ's Second Coming and living his life in accordance with Christ's will is too tied to this earth. But according to God's Word, only those believers who have an eternal perspective, who are truly heavenly minded, can be of service to Him on earth, because they are freed from the earthly desires and motivations that hinder the obedience of many of His children. Faithful believers are fruitful believers, and they know that their true citizenship is in heaven (Phil 3:20) and that their inheritance is a promise of God (Heb 6:12), who cannot lie and who is always faithful to fulfill His promises.

When Paul was caught up into the third heaven, he beheld sights and heard utterances that were beyond human description (2 Cor 12:2–4). Even the inspired apostle was unable to depict the grandeur, majesty, and glory of heaven. Yet every believer some day not only will behold and comprehend those divine wonders but will share fully in them.

"And everyone who has this hope fixed on Him purifies himself, just as He is pure," John tells us (1 John 3:3). The hope and expectation of sharing in God's own glory should motivate every believer to dedicate himself to living purely while he is still on earth. Only a holy life is fully usable by God, and only a holy life is rightly prepared to receive the inheritance of the Lord.

One day everything on earth will perish and disappear, because the whole earth is defiled and corrupted. By great and marvelous contrast, however, one day every believer will "obtain an inheritance which is imperishable and undefiled and will not fade away, reserved in heaven for [him]" (1 Pet 1:4). Our present earthly life as believers is merely an "introduction by faith into this grace in which we stand," and our ultimate hope and joy are "in hope of the glory of God" (Rom 5:2). Because of his constant confidence in that ultimate inheritance, Paul could say, "I know how to get along with humble means, and I also know how to live in prosperity; in any and every circumstance I have learned the secret of being filled and going hungry, both of having abundance and suffering need" (Phil 4:12). It was also in light of our ultimate divine inheritance that Jesus admonished, "Do not lay up for yourselves treasures upon earth, where moth and rust destroy, and where thieves break in and steal. But lay up for yourselves treasures in heaven, where neither moth nor rust destroys, and where thieves do not break in or steal; for where your treasure is, there will your heart be also" (Matt 6:19–21).

THE PROOF OF GLORY

if indeed we suffer with Him in order that we may also be glorified with Him. (8:17*d*)

As in the beginning of the verse, **if** does not here connote possibility but actuality, and is better rendered "because," or "inasmuch." Paul is declaring that, strange as it seems to the earthly mind, the present proof of the believer's ultimate glory comes through suffering on his Lord's behalf. Because **we suffer with Him,** we know that we will **also be glorified with Him.** Jesus closed the Beatitudes on the same note when He gave a double promise of blessing for those who are persecuted for righteousness' sake, that is, for His sake (Matt 5:10–12).

Because the present world system is under the reign of Satan, the world despises God and the people of God. It is therefore inevitable that whether persecution comes in the form of mere verbal abuse at one extreme or as martyrdom at the other extreme, no believer is exempt from the possibility of paying a price for his faith. When **we suffer** mockery, scorn, ridicule, or any other form of persecution because of our relationship to Jesus Christ, we can take that affliction as divine proof we truly belong to Christ and that our hope of heavenly glory is not in vain, that ultimately we will **also be glorified with Him.**

Many of God's promises are not what we think of as "positive." Jesus promised, "A disciple is not above his teacher, nor a slave above his master. It is enough for the disciple that he become as his teacher, and the slave as his master. If they have called the head of the house Beelzebul, how much more the members of his household!" (Matt 10:24–25). Paul promised that "all who desire to live godly in Christ Jesus will be persecuted" (2 Tim 3:12; cf. 2:11). Peter implies the same promise of persecution in his first epistle: "And after you have suffered for a little while, the God of all grace, who called you to His eternal glory in Christ, will Himself perfect, confirm, strengthen and establish you" (1 Pet 5:10). Suffering is an integral part of the process of spiritual maturity, and Peter assumes that every true believer will undergo some degree of suffering for the Lord's sake. Those who will reign with Christ in the life to come will enjoy the rewards for their suffering for Him during their life on earth.

Paul declares with confidence and joy, "We are afflicted in every way, but not crushed; perplexed, but not despairing; persecuted, but not forsaken; struck down, but not destroyed; always carrying about in the body the dying of Jesus, that the life of Jesus also may be manifested in our body. For we who live are constantly being delivered over to death for Jesus' sake, that the life of Jesus also may be manifested in our mortal flesh" (2 Cor 4:8–11). Paul was willing to suffer for the sake of his fellow believers and for the sake of those who needed to believe, but his greatest motivation for suffering was the glory his suffering brought to God. "For all things are for your sakes," he went on to say, "that the grace which is spreading to more and more people may cause the giving of thanks to abound to the glory of God" (v. 15). Yet he also willingly suffered for his own sake, because he knew that his travail for the sake of Christ would accrue to his own benefit. "Therefore we do not lose heart," he said, "but though our outer man is decaying, yet our inner man is being renewed day by day. For momentary, light affliction is producing for us an eternal weight of glory far beyond all comparison" (vv. 16–17).

The more a believer suffers in this life for the sake of his Lord, the greater will be his capacity for glory in heaven. Jesus made this relationship clear in Matthew 20:21–23, when He told James, John, and their mother that elevation to prominence in the future kingdom will be related to experiencing the depths of the cup of suffering through humiliation here and now. As with the relationship between works and rewards (see 1 Cor 3:12–15), the spiritual quality of our earthly life will, in some divinely determined way, affect the quality of our heavenly life. It should be added that since the ultimate destiny of believers is to glorify God, it seems certain that our heavenly rewards and glory in essence will be capacities for glorifying Him.

The suffering in this life creates reactions that reflect the genuine condition of the soul. God allows suffering to drive believers to dependence on Him— an evidence of their true salvation.

Suffering because of our faith not only gives evidence that we belong to God and are destined for heaven but also is a type of preparation for heaven. That is why Paul was so eager to experience "the fellowship of [Christ's] sufferings, being conformed to His death" (Phil 3:10) and was so determined to "press on toward the goal for the prize of the upward call of God in Christ Jesus" (v. 14).

The more we willingly suffer for Christ's sake on earth, the more we are driven to depend on Him rather than on our own resources and the more we are infused with His power. Suffering for Christ draws us closer to Christ. Our suffering for Him also enables us to better appreciate the sufferings He endured for our sakes during His incarnation. Whatever ridicule, rejection, ostracism, loss, imprisonment, physical pain, or type of death we may have to suffer for Christ is nothing compared to what we will gain. As already cited, these sufferings, no matter how severe they seem at the time, are no more than momentary, light afflictions which are "producing for us an eternal weight of glory far beyond all comparison" (2 Cor 4:17).

Our being born again, our being given hope through Christ's resurrection, our obtaining an imperishable inheritance with Him, and our protection by God's power give us reason to "greatly rejoice" (1 Pet 1:3–6a). The apostle then reminds his readers, however, that "now for a little while, if necessary, you have been distressed by various trials, that the proof of your faith, being more precious than gold which is perishable, even though tested by fire, may be found to result in praise and glory and honor at the revelation of Jesus Christ" (vv. 6b–7).

Our eternal capacity to glorify God in heaven will depend on our willingness to suffer for God while we are on earth. As mentioned above, persecution of some sort is not merely a possibility for true believers but an absolute certainty. "If the world hates you," Jesus assures His followers, "you know that it has hated Me before it hated you. If you were of the world, the world would love its own; but because you are not of the world, but I chose you out of the world, therefore the world hates you. Remember the word that I said to you, 'A slave is not greater than his master.' If they persecuted Me, they will also persecute you; if they kept My word, they will keep yours also. But all these things they will do to you for My name's sake, because they do not know the One who sent Me" (John 15:18–21).

To take a strong biblical stand for Christ is to guarantee some kind of opposition, alienation, affliction, and rejection by the world. Unfortunately, it also often brings criticism from those who profess to know God but by their deeds deny Him (Titus 1:16).

Yet we also have the Lord's wonderful assurance that nothing we suffer for His sake will do us any lasting harm, because "just as the sufferings of Christ are ours in abundance, so also our comfort is abundant through Christ" (2 Cor 1:5). We have no greater privilege and no greater guarantee of glory than to suffer for Christ's sake.

The so-called health and wealth and prosperity gospels that abound today are not true to the gospel of Christ but reflect the message of the world. The world's seemingly good news offers temporary escape from problems and hardship. Christ's good news includes the promise of suffering for His sake.

THE COMPARISON OF GLORY

For I consider that the sufferings of this present time are not worthy to be compared with the glory that is to be revealed to us. (8:18)

Logizomai (to **consider**) refers literally to numerical calculation. Figuratively, as it is used here, it refers to reaching a settled conclusion by careful study and reasoning. Paul does not merely suggest, but strongly affirms, that any suffering for Christ's sake is a small price to pay for the gracious benefits received because of that suffering. **The sufferings of this present time,** that is, our time on earth, **are not worthy to be compared with the glory that is to be revealed to us.**

In the New Testament, *pathēma* (**sufferings**) is used both of Christ's sufferings and of believers' suffering for His sake. Resist Satan, Peter admonishes, "firm in your faith, knowing that the same experiences of suffering are being accomplished by your brethren who are in the world" (1 Pet 5:9). Paul assured the Corinthian Christians, "If we are afflicted, it is for your comfort and salvation; or if we are comforted, it is for your comfort, which is effective in the patient enduring of the same sufferings which we also suffer; and our hope for you is firmly grounded, knowing that as you are sharers of our sufferings, so also you are sharers of our comfort" (2 Cor 1:6–7).

Jesus Christ is the supreme and perfect example of suffering for righteousness' sake. "For it was fitting for Him, for whom are all things, and through whom are all things, in bringing many sons to glory, to perfect the author of their salvation through sufferings" (Heb 2:10). Just as suffering was essential to Christ's obedience to His Father, so it is essential to our obedience to Christ.

Those who do not know Christ have no hope when they suffer. Whatever the reason for their affliction, it does not come upon them for Christ's sake, or righteousness's sake, and therefore cannot produce for them any spiritual blessing or glory. Those who live only for this life cannot look forward to any resolution of wrongs or to any comfort for their souls. Their pain, loneliness, and afflictions serve no divine purpose and bring no divine reward.

Christians, on the other hand, have great hope, not only that their afflictions eventually will end but that those afflictions actually will add to their eternal glory. Long before the incarnation of Christ, the prophet Daniel spoke of believers' glory as "the brightness of the expanse of heaven," and as being "like the stars forever and ever" (Dan 12:3).

As followers of Christ, our suffering comes from men, whereas our glory comes from God. Our suffering is earthly, whereas our glory is heavenly. Our suffering is short, whereas our glory is forever. Our suffering is trivial, whereas our glory is limitless. Our suffering is in our mortal and corrupted bodies, whereas our glory will be in our perfected and imperishable bodies.

05

THE HOLY SPIRIT GUARANTEES OUR GLORY—PART 2 THE INEXPRESSIBLE GROANS FOR GLORY

ROMANS 8:19-27

For the anxious longing of the creation waits eagerly for the revealing of the sons of God. For the creation was subjected to futility, not of its own will, but because of Him who subjected it, in hope that the creation itself also will be set free from its slavery to corruption into the freedom of the glory of the children of God. For we know that the whole creation groans and suffers the pains of childbirth together until now. And not only this, but also we ourselves, having the first fruits of the Spirit, even we ourselves groan within ourselves, waiting eagerly for our adoption as sons, the redemption of our body. For in hope we have been saved, but hope that is seen is not hope; for why does one also hope for what he sees? But if we hope for what we do not see, with perseverance we wait eagerly for it.

And in the same way the Spirit also helps our weakness; for we do not know how to pray as we should, but the Spirit Himself intercedes for us with groanings too deep for words; and He who searches the hearts knows what the mind of the Spirit is, because He intercedes for the saints according to the will of God. (8:19–27)

In his climactic presentation of the ministry of the Holy Spirit in securing the no-condemnation status of believers (see 8:1), Paul focuses on His securing us by guaranteeing our future glory (vv. 17–30). In the previous chapter of this volume we studied the incomparable gains that believers possess because of their God-promised glory (vv. 17–18).

In the present chapter Paul focuses our attention on the anticipation of that glory—the incomparable groans—of creation (vv. 19–22), of believers (vv. 23–25), and of the Holy Spirit Himself (vv. 26–27). A groan is an audible expression of anguish due to physical, emotional, or spiritual pain. These groanings bewail a condition that is painful, unsatisfying, and sorrowful—a cry for deliverance from a torturing experience.

THE GROANING OF CREATION

For the anxious longing of the creation waits eagerly for the revealing of the sons of God. For the creation was subjected to futility, not of its own will, but because of Him who subjected it, in hope that the creation itself also will be set free from its slavery to corruption into the freedom of the glory of the children of God. For we know that the whole creation groans and suffers the pains of childbirth together until now. (8:19–22)

The first groan is the personified lament coming from the created universe as it now exists in the corrupted condition caused by the Fall.

THE TRIUMPH OF LOVE

Apokaradokia (**anxious longing**) is an especially vivid word that literally refers to watching with outstretched head, and suggests standing on tiptoes with the eyes looking ahead with intent expectancy. The prefix *apo* adds the idea of fixed absorption and concentration on that which is anticipated. **The creation** is standing on tiptoes, as it were, as it **waits eagerly for the revealing of the sons of God.**

Jews were familiar with God's promise of a redeemed world, a renewed **creation.** On behalf of the Lord, Isaiah predicted, "For behold, I create new heavens and a new earth; and the former things shall not be remembered or come to mind" (Isa 65:17). Jews anticipated a glorious time when all pain, oppression, slavery, anxiety, sorrow, and persecution would end and the Lord would establish His own perfect kingdom of peace and righteousness.

Even nonbiblical Jewish writings reflect that longing. The Apocalypse of Baruch describes an expected and long-awaited future utopia:

> The vine shall yield its fruit ten thousand fold, and on each vine there shall be a thousand branches; and each branch shall produce a thousand clusters; and each cluster produce a thousand grapes; and each grape a cor of wine. And those who have hungered shall rejoice; moreover, also, they shall behold marvels every day. For winds shall go forth from before me to bring every morning the fragrance of aromatic fruits, and at the close of the day clouds distilling the dews of health. (29:5)

Jewish sections of Sibylline Oracles record similar expectations. "And earth, and all the trees, and the innumerable flocks of sheep shall give their true fruit to mankind, of wine and of sweet honey and of white milk and of corn, which to men is the most excellent gift of all" (3:620–33). Later in the oracles it says,

> Earth, the universal mother, shall give to mortals her best fruit in countless store of corn, wine and oil. Yea, from heaven shall come a sweet draught of luscious honey. The trees shall yield their proper fruits, and rich flocks, and kine, and lambs of sheep and kids of goats. He will cause sweet fountains of white milk to burst forth. And the cities shall be full of good things, and the fields rich; neither shall there be any sword throughout the land or battle-din; nor shall the earth be convulsed any more, nor shall there be any more drought throughout the land, no famine, or hail to work havoc on the crops. (3:744–56)

Creation does not here include the heavenly angels, who, although created beings, are not subject to corruption. The term obviously does not include Satan and his host of fallen angels, the demons. They have no desire for a godly, sinless state and know they are divinely sentenced to eternal torment. Believers are not included in that term either, because they are mentioned separately in verses 23–25. Nor is Paul referring to unbelievers. The only remaining part of **creation** is the nonrational part, including animals and plants and all inanimate things such as the mountains, rivers, plains, seas, and heavenly bodies.

Jews were familiar with such a personification of nature. Isaiah had used it when he wrote that "The wilderness and the desert will be glad, and the Arabah will rejoice and blossom" (Isa 35:1), and later that "the mountains and the hills will break forth into shouts of joy before you, and all the trees of the field will clap their hands" (55:12).

Waits eagerly translates a form of the verb *apekdechomai*, which refers to waiting in great anticipation but with patience. The form of the Greek verb gives the added connotations of readiness, preparedness, and continuance until the expected event occurs.

Revealing translates *apokalupsis*, which refers to an uncovering, unveiling, or revelation. It is this word from which the English name of the book of Revelation is derived (see Rev 1:1). The world does not comprehend who Christians really are. In his first epistle, John explained to fellow believers: "See how great a love the Father has bestowed upon us, that we should be called children of God; and such we are. For this reason the world does not know us, because it did not know Him" (1 John 3:1).

In the present age, the world is unable to distinguish absolutely between Christians and nonbelievers. People who call themselves Christians walk, dress, and talk much like everyone else. Many unbelievers have high standards of behavior. On the other hand, unfortunately, many professing Christians give little evidence of salvation. But at the appointed time God will reveal those who are truly His.

At **the revealing of the sons of God,** "when Christ, who is our life, is revealed, then [believers] also will be revealed with Him in glory" (Col 3:4). At that time, all believers will be eternally separated from sin and their unredeemed humanness, to be glorified with Christ's own holiness and splendor.

When Adam and Eve sinned by disobeying God's command, not only mankind but the earth and all the rest of the world was cursed and corrupted. After the Fall, God said to Adam,

> Because you have listened to the voice of your wife, and have eaten from the tree about which I commanded you, saying, "You shall not eat from it"; cursed is the ground because of you; in toil you shall eat of it all the days of your life. Both thorns and thistles it shall grow for you; and you shall eat the plants of the field; by the sweat of your face you shall eat bread, till you return to the ground, because from it you were taken; for you are dust, and to dust you shall return. (Gen 3:17–19)

Before the Fall, no weeds or poisonous plants, no thorns or thistles or anything else existed that could cause man misery or harm. But after the Fall, **the**

creation was subjected to futility, not of its own will, but because of Him who subjected it. *Mataiotēs* (**futility**) carries the idea of being without success, of being unable to achieve a goal or purpose. Because of man's sin, no part of nature now exists as God intended it to be and as it originally was. The verb **was subjected** indicates by its form that nature did not curse itself but was cursed by something or someone else. Paul goes on to reveal that the curse on nature was executed by its Creator. God Himself **subjected it** to futility.

Although various environmental organizations and government agencies today make noble attempts to protect and restore natural resources and regions, they are helpless to turn the tide of corruption that has continually devastated both man and his environment since the Fall. Such is the destructiveness of sin that one man's disobedience brought corruption to the entire universe. Decay, disease, pain, death, natural disaster, pollution, and all other forms of evil will never cease until the One who sent the curse removes it and creates a new heaven and a new earth (2 Pet 3:13; Rev 21:1).

No less a naturalist than John Muir was in serious error when he wrote that nature is "unfallen and undepraved" and that only man is a "blighting touch." The sentimental environmentalists of our time advocate living in some relaxed and easy "harmony with nature." Some are crying for the government to take us back to living in the Dark Ages, when, they assume, people and nature were in harmony. All the corruptions of this fallen environment were different in the past from what technology and industry have wrought—but perhaps even more deadly. Certainly disease and death, as well as exposure to the natural elements and disasters, were much greater in the past. And when people were supposedly living nearer nature, they had less comfort, more pain, harder times, more disease, and died younger. This is not a friendly earth but a violent and dangerous one. It is a ridiculous fantasy to think it is not cursed and that it naturally yields a comfortable life.

In spite of this curse, however, much of the beauty, grandeur, and benefits of the natural world remains. Although they all deteriorate, flowers are still beautiful, mountains are still grand, forests are still magnificent, the heavenly bodies are still majestic, food still brings nourishment and is a pleasure to eat, and water still brings refreshment and sustains life. Despite the terrible curse that He inflicted on the earth, God's majesty and gracious provision for mankind is still evident wherever one looks. It is for that reason that no person has an excuse for not believing in God: "Since the creation of the world His invisible attributes, His eternal power and divine nature, have been clearly seen, being understood through what has been made, so that they are without excuse" (Rom 1:20).

Nature's destiny is inseparably linked to man's. Because man sinned, the rest of **creation** was corrupted with him. Likewise, when man's glory is divinely restored, the natural world will be restored as well. Therefore, Paul says, there is **hope** even for the natural creation itself, which **will be set free from its slavery to corruption into the freedom of the glory of the children of God.** In other words, just as man's sin brought corruption to the universe, so man's restoration to righteousness will be accompanied by the restoration of the earth and its universe to their divinely-intended perfection and glory.

In physics, the law of entropy refers to the constant and irreversible degradation of matter and energy in the universe to increasing disorder, that scientific law clearly contradicts the theory of evolution, which is based on the premise that the natural world is inclined to continual self-improvement. But it is evident even in a simple garden plot that, when it is untended, it deteriorates. Weeds and other undesirable plants will choke out the good ones. The natural bent of the universe—whether of humans, animals, plants, or the inanimate elements of the earth and heavens—is obviously and demonstrably downward, not upward. It could not be otherwise while the world remains in **slavery to the corruption** of sin.

Yet despite their continual corruption and degeneration, neither man nor the universe itself will bring about their ultimate destruction. That is in the province of God alone, and there is no need to fear an independently initiated human holocaust. Men need fear only the God whom they rebelliously spurn and oppose. The destiny of earth is entirely in the hands of its Creator, and that destiny includes God's total destruction of the sin-cursed universe. "The day of the Lord will come like a thief, in which the heavens will pass away with a roar and the elements will be destroyed with intense heat, and the earth and its works will be burned up" (2 Pet 3:10). That destruction will be on a scale infinitely more powerful than any man-made devices could achieve.

In his vision on Patmos, John "saw a new heaven and a new earth; for the first heaven and the first earth passed away, and there is no longer any sea.... And [God] shall wipe away every tear from their eyes; and there shall no longer be any death; there shall no longer be any mourning, or crying, or pain; the first things have passed away. And He who sits on the throne said, 'Behold, I am making all things new.' And He said, 'Write, for these words are faithful and true'" (Rev 21:1, 4–5).

It is for that promised time of redemption and restoration that all nature groans in hope and expectation. As with "was subjected" in the previous verse, the verb **will be set free** is passive, indicating that nature will not restore itself but will be restored by God, who Himself long ago subjected it to corruption and futility.

Jesus referred to that awesome time as "the regeneration," a time when the old sinful environment will be radically judged and be replaced with God's new and righteous one. "Truly I say to you," He told the disciples, "that you who have followed Me, in the regeneration when the Son of Man will sit on His glorious throne, you also shall sit upon twelve thrones, judging the twelve tribes of Israel" (Matt 19:28).

The freedom of the glory of the children of God refers to the time when all believers will be liberated from sin, liberated from the flesh, and liberated from their humanness. At that time we will begin to share eternally in God's own **glory,** with which **God** will clothe all His precious **children.** John reminds us, "Beloved, now we are children of God, and it has not appeared as yet what we shall be. We know that, when He appears, we shall be like Him, because we shall see Him just as He is" (1 John 3:2). In describing that glorious day, Paul wrote,

> Behold, I tell you a mystery; we shall not all sleep, but we shall all be changed, in a moment, in the twinkling of an eye, at the last trumpet; for the trumpet will sound, and the dead will be raised imperishable, and we shall be changed. For this perishable must put on the imperishable, and this mortal must put on immortality. But when this perishable will have put on the imperishable, and this mortal will have put on immortality, then will come about the saying that is written, "Death is swallowed up in victory." (1 Cor 15:51–54)

It is impossible for our finite minds to comprehend such divine mysteries. But by God's own Holy Spirit within us we can believe all of His revealed truth and rejoice with absolute and confident hope that our eternal life with our Father in heaven is secure. We acknowledge with Paul that "our citizenship is in heaven, from which also we eagerly wait for a Savior, the Lord Jesus Christ; who will transform the body of our humble state into conformity with the body of His glory, by the exertion of the power that He has even to subject all things to Himself" (Phil 3:20–21).

We also acknowledge with the apostle that nature also awaits with hope for our redemption, a redemption it will share with us in its own way. But until that wonderful day and in anticipation of it, **the whole creation groans and suffers the pains of childbirth together until now.**

Stenazō (**groans**) refers to the utterances of a person who is caught in a dreadful situation and has no immediate prospect of deliverance. The term is used in its noun form by Luke to describe the desperate utterances of the Israelites during their bondage in Egypt (Acts 7:34). The verb is used by the writer of Hebrews to describe the frustration and grief of church leaders caused by immature and unruly members (13:17).

The groaning and suffering of the **creation** will one day cease, because God will deliver it from its corruption and futility. In the meanwhile, it endures **the pains of childbirth.** Like Eve, whose sin brought the curse of painful human childbirth (Gen 3:16), nature endures its own kind of labor pains. But also like

Eve and her descendants, nature's **pains of childbirth** presage new life.

Paul makes no mention of how or when the world will be made new. Nor does he give the phases of that cosmic regeneration or the sequence of events. Many other passages of Scripture shed light on the details of the curses being lifted (see Isa 30:23–24; 35:1–7; etc.) and the ultimate creation of a new heaven and a new earth (2 Pet 3:13; Rev 21:1), but Paul's purpose here is to assure his readers in general terms that God's master plan of redemption encompasses the entire universe.

D. Martyn Lloyd-Jones wrote with deep insight:

> I wonder whether the phenomenon of the Spring supplies us with a part answer. Nature every year, as it were, makes an effort to renew itself, to produce something permanent; it has come out of the death and the darkness of all that is so true of the Winter. In the Spring it seems to be trying to produce a perfect creation, to be going through some kind of birth-pangs year by year. But unfortunately it does not succeed, for Spring leads only to Summer, whereas Summer leads to Autumn, and Autumn to Winter. Poor old nature tries every year to defeat the "vanity," the principle of death and decay and disintegration that is in it. But it cannot do so. It fails every time. It still goes on trying, as if it feels things should be different and better; but it never succeeds. So it goes on "groaning and travailing in pain together until now." It has been doing so for a very long time ... but nature still repeats the effort annually. (Romans [Grand Rapids: Zondervan, 1980], 6:59–60)

THE GROANING OF BELIEVERS

And not only this, but also we ourselves, having the first fruits of the Spirit, even we ourselves groan within ourselves, waiting eagerly for our adoption as sons, the redemption of our body. For in hope we have been saved, but hope that is seen is not hope; for why does one also hope for what he sees? But if we hope for what we do not see, with perseverance we wait eagerly for it. (8:23–25)

Not only does the natural creation groan for deliverance from the destructive consequences of sin into the promised new universe, **but also we ourselves,** that is, believers. It is the redemption of believers that is central to God's ultimate cosmic regeneration, because believers— as His own children, redeemed and adopted into His heavenly family in response to their faith in His beloved Son, Jesus Christ—are the heirs of His glorious, eternal, and righteous kingdom.

Every true believer agonizes at times over the appalling manifestations and consequences of sin— in his own life, in the lives of others, and even in the natural world. Because we have **the first fruits of the Spirit,** we are spiritually sensitized to the corruption of sin in and around us.

Because the Holy **Spirit** now indwells us, His work in us and through us is a type of spiritual **first fruits.**

They are a foretaste of the glory that awaits us in heaven, when our corrupted and mortal bodies are exchanged for ones that are incorruptible and immortal. Although we will not be totally free of sin's power as long as we are in our present bodies, the Lord has given us complete victory over the dominion and bondage of sin. When we experience the Holy Spirit's empowering us to turn from iniquity and to truly worship, serve, obey, and love God, we have a taste of the future completed and perfected renewal He will work in us at the resurrection.

Because every genuine believer is indwelt by the Holy Spirit (Rom 8:9), every genuine believer will to some degree manifest the fruit of the Spirit that Paul enumerates in Galatians 5:22–23, namely, "love, joy, peace, patience, kindness, goodness, faithfulness, gentleness, self-control." Every time we see Him working His righteousness in and through us, we yearn all the more to be freed of our remaining sin and spiritual weakness. Because of our divinely bestowed sensitivity to sin, **we ourselves groan within ourselves** over the dreadful curse of sin that is still manifested by our remaining humanness.

Acknowledging his own sinfulness, David cried out, "My iniquities are gone over my head; as a heavy burden they weigh too much for me.... Lord, all my desire is before Thee; and my sighing is not hidden from Thee. My heart throbs, my strength fails me; and the light of my eyes, even that has gone from me" (Ps 38:4, 9–10).

Paul grieved over the remnants of his humanness that clung to him like a rotten garment that could not be cast off. That reality brought him great spiritual frustration and anguish. "Wretched man that I am!" he lamented, "Who will set me free from the body of this death?" (Rom 7:24). In another epistle he reminds all believers of their same plight: "For indeed while we are in this tent, we groan, being burdened, because we do not want to be unclothed, but to be clothed, in order that what is mortal may be swallowed up by life" (2 Cor 5:4). As long as we are in the "tent" of our human body, we will never fully escape sin's corruption in our lives. That truth causes Christians to suffer times of deep inner distress over the debilitating sinfulness that still clings to them.

As believers, we therefore find ourselves **waiting eagerly** in anticipation of **our adoption as sons, the redemption of our body.** The New Testament speaks of believers as those who are already the adopted children of God, but whose adoption awaits ultimate perfection. Just as there is never salvation that is not completed, neither is there divine adoption that is not completed. A child of God need never fear that he might be cast out of his spiritual family or never enter his heavenly home.

Puritan pastor Thomas Watson said,

> The godly may act faintly in religion, the pulse of their affections may beat low. The exercise of grace may be hindered,

as when the course of water is stopped. Instead of grace working in the godly, corruption may work; instead of patience, murmuring; instead of heavenliness, earthliness.... Thus lively and vigorous may corruption be in the regenerate; they may fall into enormous sins.... [But] though their grace may be drawn low, it is not drawn dry; though grace may be abated, it is not abolished.... Grace may suffer an eclipse, not a dissolution.... A believer may fall from some degrees of grace, but not from the state of grace. (*A Body of Divinity* [reprint, Edinburgh: Banner of Truth, 1974], pp. 280, 284–85)

Scripture teaches that the believer's salvation is secured by God the Father, by the Son, and by the Holy Spirit. Referring to God the Father, Paul assured the Corinthians, "He who establishes us with you in Christ and anointed us is God, who also sealed us and gave us the Spirit in our hearts as a pledge" (2 Cor 1:21–22; cf. 2 Tim 2:19). The Father not only grants salvation to those who trust in His Son but also seals their salvation and gives the indwelling Holy Spirit as the guarantor. "Blessed be the God and Father of our Lord Jesus Christ," Peter declared, "who according to His great mercy has caused us to be born again to a living hope through the resurrection of Jesus Christ from the dead, to obtain an inheritance which is imperishable and undefiled and will not fade away, reserved in heaven for you, who are protected by the power of God through faith for a salvation ready to be revealed in the last time" (1 Pet 1:3–5). Although persevering faith is indispensable to salvation, Peter emphasizes that, by God the Father's own initiative and power, He "caused us to be born again" and in that same power He sustains us toward the inheritance that our new birth brings, an inheritance that is "imperishable and undefiled and will not fade away." It is divinely "reserved in heaven" for each believer, who is divinely preserved to receive it. Whoever belongs to God belongs to Him forever.

In order to point up the absolute and incontrovertible security of those who trust in Jesus Christ, the writer of Hebrews declared, "In the same way God, desiring even more to show to the heirs of the promise the unchangeableness of His purpose, interposed with an oath, in order that by two unchangeable things, in which it is impossible for God to lie, we may have strong encouragement, we who have fled for refuge in laying hold of the hope set before us. This hope we have as an anchor of the soul, a hope both sure and steadfast and one which enters within the veil" (Heb 6:17–19).

God the Son also secures the believer's salvation. "All that the Father gives Me shall come to Me," Jesus declared, "and the one who comes to Me I will certainly not cast out" (John 6:37). Paul assured the Corinthian church, which had more than its share of immature and disobedient believers, that "even as the testimony concerning Christ was confirmed in you, so that you are not lacking in any gift, awaiting eagerly the revelation of our Lord Jesus Christ, who shall also confirm you to the end, blameless in the day of our Lord Jesus Christ" (1 Cor 1:6–8; cf. Col 1:22). In other words, their relationship to Christ not only had been confirmed when they were justified but would remain confirmed by the Lord Himself until their glorification at His return (cf. 1 Thess 3:13). Later in that epistle Paul reminds us that "faithful is He who calls you, and He also will bring it to pass" (1 Thess 5:24). The ongoing, mediatorial, intercessory work of Jesus Christ in heaven unalterably secures our eternal reward.

God the Spirit also secures the believer's salvation, by a work that Scripture sometimes refers to as the Spirit's sealing. In ancient times, the seal, or signet, was a mark of authenticity or of a completed transaction. The seal of a monarch or other distinguished person represented his authority and power. For example, when Daniel was thrown into the den of lions, King Darius had a large stone placed across the entrance and sealed "with his own signet ring and with the signet rings of his nobles, so that nothing might be changed in regard to Daniel" (Dan 6:17). In an infinitely more significant and spiritual way, the Holy Spirit seals the salvation of every believer, which, by divine promise and protection, can never be altered.

Paul assured the Corinthian believers that "He who establishes us with you in Christ and anointed us is God, who also sealed us and gave us the Spirit in our hearts as a pledge" (2 Cor 1:21–22). In similar words, he assured the Ephesians that "In Him [Christ], you also, after listening to the message of truth, the gospel of your salvation—having also believed, you were sealed in Him with the Holy Spirit of promise" (Eph 1:13; cf. 4:30).

The ideas of partial or temporary salvation not only are foreign to the teaching of Scripture but completely contradict it. No true believer need ever fear loss of salvation. At the moment of conversion his soul is redeemed, purified, and eternally secured in God's family and kingdom.

Believers should be concerned about sin in their lives, but not because they might sin themselves out of God's grace. Because of God's promise and power, that is impossible. Until we are glorified and fully liberated from sin through **the redemption of our body,** we still have unredeemed bodies that make it very much possible for sin to harm us and to grieve our Lord. As the term is often used in the New Testament, **body** is not limited to a person's physical being but relates to the whole of his unredeemed humanness, in particular to the remaining susceptibility to sin.

It is only the **body,** the mortal humanness of a believer, that is yet to be redeemed. The inner person is already a completely new creation, a partaker of God's nature and indwelt by God's Spirit. "Therefore if any man is in Christ," Paul says, "he is a new creature; the old things passed away; behold, new things have come"

(2 Cor 5:17). Peter assures us that God's "divine power has granted to us everything pertaining to life and godliness, through the true knowledge of Him who called us by His own glory and excellence. For by these He has granted to us His precious and magnificent promises, in order that by them you might become partakers of the divine nature, having escaped the corruption that is in the world by lust" (2 Pet 1:3–4).

Because believers are already new creatures possessing the divine nature, their souls are fit for heaven and eternal glory. They love God, hate sin, and have holy longings for obedience to the Word. But while on earth they are kept in bondage by their mortal bodies, which are still corrupted by sin and its consequences. Christians are holy seeds, as it were, encased in an unholy shell. Incarcerated in a prison of flesh and subjected to its weaknesses and imperfections, we therefore eagerly await an event that is divinely guaranteed but is yet to transpire—the **redemption of our body.**

Paul has already explained that "if we [believers] have become united with Him [Christ] in the likeness of His death, certainly we shall be also in the likeness of His resurrection, knowing this, that our old self was crucified with Him, that our body of sin might be done away with, that we should no longer be slaves to sin" (Rom 6:5–6). The old man with his old sinful nature is dead, but the corrupted **body** in which he dwelt is still present. That is why, a few verses later,

Paul admonishes believers not to "let sin reign in your mortal body that you should obey its lusts" and not to "go on presenting the members of your body to sin as instruments of unrighteousness; but present yourselves to God as those alive from the dead, and your members as instruments of righteousness to God" (vv. 12–13). Because we are still capable of sinning, we should be continually on guard to resist and overcome sin in the Spirit's power (vv. 14–17).

Paul also has already explained "that the Law is spiritual; but I am of flesh, sold into bondage to sin. For that which I am doing, I do not understand; for I am not practicing what I would like to do, but I am doing the very thing I hate" (Rom 7:14–15). "But if I do the very thing I do not wish to do," he continues, "I agree with the Law, confessing that it is good. So now, no longer am I the one doing it, but sin which indwells me. For I know that nothing good dwells in me, that is, in my flesh; for the wishing is present in me, but the doing of the good is not" (vv. 16–18).

It is encouragingly hopeful for Christians to realize that their falling into sin does not have its source in their deepest inner being, their new and holy nature in Christ. When they sin, they do so because of the desires and promptings of the flesh—that is, their bodies, their remaining humanness—which they cannot escape until they go to be with the Lord. Summing up that vital truth, Paul said, "Thanks be to God through Jesus Christ our

Lord! So then, on the one hand I myself with my mind am serving the law of God, but on the other, with my flesh the law of sin" (Rom 7:25).

As noted above, our souls are already fully redeemed and are fit for heaven. But the fleshly, outer clothing of the old, sinful person is still corrupted and awaits redemption. "For our citizenship is in heaven," Paul explains, "from which also we eagerly wait for a Savior, the Lord Jesus Christ; who will transform the body of our humble state into conformity with the body of His glory, by the exertion of the power that He has even to subject all things to Himself" (Phil 3:20–21).

It is hardly possible not to wonder what kind of resurrected and redeemed body believers will have in heaven, but it is foolish to speculate about it apart from what Scripture teaches. Anticipating such curiosity, Paul told the Corinthians:

> Someone will say, "How are the dead raised? And with what kind of body do they come?" You fool! That which you sow does not come to life unless it dies; and that which you sow, you do not sow the body which is to be, but a bare grain, perhaps of wheat or of something else. But God gives it a body just as He wished, and to each of the seeds a body of its own. All flesh is not the same flesh, but there is one flesh of men, and another flesh of beasts, and another flesh of birds, and another of fish. There are also heavenly bodies and earthly bodies, but the glory of the heavenly is one, and the glory of the earthly is another. There is one glory of the

sun, and another glory of the moon, and another glory of
the stars; for star differs from star in glory. (1 Cor 15:35–41)

Paul's point in the first analogy is that a seed bears
no resemblance to the plant or tree into which it will
grow. As far as size is concerned, some relatively large
seeds produce small plants, whereas some smaller
seeds produce large trees. Many different kinds of seed
look much alike, and the total variety of seeds has yet
to be calculated. If given a handful of seeds that were
all different and came from various parts of the world,
not even an experienced farmer, much less the average
person, could identify all of them. Not until it is sown
and the resulting plant begins to mature can the kind
of seed be accurately identified. The same principle
applies in relation to our natural and spiritual bodies.
We cannot possibly determine what our future spiritual
bodies will be like by looking at our present physical
bodies. We will have to wait to see.

Paul also points out the obvious fact that animate
creatures vary widely in their appearance and nature, and
that, without exception, like produces like. The genetic
code of every living species is distinct and unique. No
amount of attempted interbreeding or change of diet
can turn a fish into a bird, or a horse into a dog or cat.

There is also variety in the heavenly bodies, an
immeasurably greater variety than people in Paul's day
were aware of. The apostle's point in mentioning the

animals and heavenly bodies seems to be that of calling attention to the vast magnitude and variation of God's creation and to the inability of man even to come close to comprehending it.

The Bible discloses very little about the nature of a believer's resurrected body. Paul goes on to tell the Corinthians, "So also is the resurrection of the dead. It is sown a perishable body, it is raised an imperishable body; it is sown in dishonor, it is raised in glory; it is sown in weakness, it is raised in power; it is sown a natural body, it is raised a spiritual body. If there is a natural body, there is also a spiritual body" (1 Cor 15:42–44).

Because we will ultimately be like Christ, we know that our resurrected bodies will be like His. As noted above, Paul assures us that, "if we have become united with Him in the likeness of His death, certainly we shall be also in the likeness of His resurrection" (Rom 6:5). In his epistle to Philippi he explains further that our Lord "will transform the body of our humble state into conformity with the body of His glory, by the exertion of the power that He has even to subject all things to Himself" (Phil 3:21).

During the period between His resurrection and ascension, Jesus' body still bore the physical marks of His crucifixion (John 20:20) and He was able to eat (Luke 24:30). He still looked like Himself, yet even His closest disciples could not recognize Him unless He allowed them to (Luke 24:13–16, 30–31;

John 20:14–16). He could be touched and felt (John 20:17, 27), yet He could appear and disappear in an instant and could pass through closed doors (John 20:19, 26).

Although our redeemed bodies will in some way be like Christ's, we will not know exactly what they will be like until we meet our Savior face to face (1 John 3:2). Paul's primary purpose in 1 Corinthians 15 and Romans 8 is to emphasize that our resurrected bodies, regardless of their form, appearance, or capabilities, will be sinless, righteous, and immortal.

He continues to explain that **in hope we have been saved. Hope** is inseparable from salvation. Our salvation was planned by God in ages past, bestowed in the present, and is now characterized by **hope** for its future completion.

The believer's **hope** is not based on wishful thinking or probability, but on the integrity of the clear promises of the Lord. As already cited above, "All that the Father gives Me shall come to Me," Jesus declared, "and the one who comes to Me I will certainly not cast out" (John 6:37). Our hope is not that we might not lose our salvation but that, by our Lord's own guarantee, we *cannot* and *will not* lose it.

The writer of Hebrews assures us that "God, desiring even more to show to the heirs of the promise the unchangeableness of His purpose, interposed with an oath, in order that by two unchangeable things, in which it is impossible for God to lie, we may have strong encouragement, we who have fled for refuge in laying hold of the hope set before us. This hope we have as an anchor of the soul, a hope both sure and steadfast and one which enters within the veil" (Heb 6:17–19). Paul refers to our hope of salvation as a helmet, symbolizing our divine protection from the blows of doubt that Satan sends to crush our hope (1 Thess 5:8).

As Jesus made clear in the parable of the wheat and tares (Matt 13) and in the story of the fruitless branches (John 15), there will always be some who bear the name of Christ who do not genuinely belong to Him. And, by the same token, there are true believers whose lives sometimes give little evidence of salvation. But as we shall continue to see to the end of this chapter, the Word of God is unequivocal in declaring that everyone who is saved by Jesus Christ will forever belong to Him. Although it is quite possible for a sinful Christian to struggle with the assurance of salvation and with the joy and comfort which that assurance brings, it is not possible for him to lose salvation itself.

It is true, on the other hand, that the completion of our salvation is presently a **hope** and not yet a reality. Explaining the obvious, Paul states the axiomatic truth that **hope that is seen is not hope; for why does one also hope for what he sees?** In other words, in this life we cannot expect to experience the reality of our glorification but only the **hope** of it. But since the believer's **hope** is based on God's promise, the completion of his salvation is more certain by far than anything he sees with his eyes. As we shall see later, the believer's salvation is so secure that his glorification is spoken of in the past tense (see Rom 8:30).

Therefore, Paul continues, **if we hope for what we do not see, with perseverance we wait eagerly for it.** "For I am confident of this very thing," Paul assured the Philippian believers, "that He who began a good work in you will perfect it until the day of Christ Jesus" (Phil 1:6). Because salvation is completely God's work and because He cannot lie, it is absolutely impossible for us to lose what He has given us and promises never to take away. It is in light of that absolute certainty that Peter admonishes: "Gird your minds for action, keep sober in spirit, fix your hope completely on the grace to be brought to you at the revelation of Jesus Christ" (1 Pet 1:13). It is for their faithfully holding to that hope that Paul commends the Thessalonians, assuring them that he, Silvanus, and Timothy were "constantly bearing in mind [their] work of faith and labor of love and steadfastness of hope in our Lord Jesus Christ in the presence of our God and Father, knowing, brethren beloved by God, His choice of you" (1 Thess 1:3–4). In other words, our certainty of salvation does not rest in our choosing God but in His choosing us, even "before the foundation of the world" (Eph 1:4).

THE GROANING OF THE HOLY SPIRIT

And in the same way the Spirit also helps our weakness; for we do not know how to pray as we should, but the Spirit Himself intercedes for us with groanings too deep for words; and He who searches the hearts knows what the mind of the Spirit is, because He intercedes for the saints according to the will of God. (8:26–27)

In the same way refers back to the groans of the creation and of believers for redemption from the corruption and defilement of sin. Here Paul reveals the immeasurably comforting truth that the Holy Spirit comes alongside us and all creation in groaning for God's ultimate day of restoration and His eternal reign of righteousness.

Because of our remaining humanness and susceptibility to sin and doubt, the Holy **Spirit also helps** us in **our weakness.** In this context, **weakness** doubtless refers to our human condition in general, not to specific **weaknesses.** The point is that, even after salvation, we are characterized by spiritual weakness. Acting morally, speaking the truth, witnessing for the Lord, or doing any other good thing happens only by the power of **the Spirit** working in and through us despite our human limitations.

Several times in his letter to the Philippians Paul beautifully pictures that divine-human relationship. Speaking of his own needs, he said, "I know that this shall turn out for my deliverance through your prayers and the provision of the Spirit of Jesus Christ" (Phil 1:19). **The Spirit** supplies us with all we need to be faithful, effective, and protected children of God. In the following chapter he admonishes, "So then, my beloved, just as you have always obeyed, not as in my presence only, but now much more in my absence, work out your salvation with fear and trembling; for it is God who is at work in you, both to will and to work for His good pleasure" (Phil 2:12–13). The Spirit of God works unrelentingly in us to do what we could never do alone—bring about the perfect will of God.

To make clear how the Spirit works, Paul turns to the subject of prayer. Although we are redeemed and absolutely secure in our adoption as God's children, nevertheless **we do not know how to pray as we should.** Paul does not elaborate on our inability to pray as we ought, but his statement is all-encompassing. Because of our imperfect perspectives, finite minds, human frailties, and spiritual limitations, we are not able to pray in absolute consistency with God's will. Many times we are not even aware that spiritual needs exist, much less know how best they should be met. Even the Christian who prays sincerely, faithfully, and regularly cannot possibly know God's purposes concerning all of his own needs or the needs of others for whom he prays.

Jesus told Peter, "Behold, Satan has demanded permission to sift you like wheat; but I have prayed for you, that your faith may not fail; and you, when once you have turned again, strengthen your brothers" (Luke 22:31–32). Fortunately for Peter, Jesus kept His word despite the apostle's foolish bravado. Not only was Peter no match for Satan but he soon proved that his devotion to Christ could not even withstand the taunts of a few strangers (vv. 54–60). How glorious that our spiritual security rests in the Lord's faithfulness rather than in our vacillating commitment.

Even the apostle Paul, who lived so near to God and so faithfully and sacrificially proclaimed His gospel, did not always know how best to pray. He knew, for example, that God had allowed Satan to inflict him with an unspecified "thorn in the flesh." That affliction guarded Paul against pride over being "caught up into Paradise." But after a while Paul became weary of the infirmity, which doubtless was severe, and he prayed earnestly that it might be removed. After three entreaties, the Lord told Paul that he should be satisfied with the abundance of divine grace by which he was already sustained in the trial (see 2 Cor 12:3–9). Paul's request did not correspond to the Lord's will for him at that time. Even when we do not know what God wants, the indwelling **Spirit**

Himself intercedes for us, bringing our needs before God even when we do not know what they are or when we pray about them unwisely.

Paul emphasizes that our help is from **the Spirit Himself.** His divine help not only is personal but direct. **The Spirit** does not simply provide our security but is **Himself** our security. The Spirit intercedes on our behalf in a way, Paul says, that is totally beyond human comprehension, **with groanings too deep for words.** The Holy Spirit unites with us in our desire to be freed from our corrupted earthly bodies and to be with God forever in our glorified heavenly bodies.

Contrary to the interpretation of most charismatics, the **groanings** of the Spirit are not utterances in unknown tongues, much less ecstatic gibberish that has no rational content. As Paul says explicitly, the groans are not even audible and are inexpressible in **words.** Yet those groans carry profound content, namely divine appeals for the spiritual welfare of each believer. In a way infinitely beyond our understanding, these **groanings** represent what might be called intertrinitarian communication, divine articulations by the Holy Spirit to the Father. Paul affirmed this truth to the Corinthians when he declared, "For who among men knows the thoughts of a man except the spirit of the man, which is in him? Even so the thoughts of God no one knows except the Spirit of God" (1 Cor 2:11).

We remain justified and righteous before God the Father only because the Son and the Holy Spirit, as our constant advocates and intercessors, represent us before Him. It is only because of that joint and unceasing divine work on our behalf that we will enter heaven. Christ "is able to save forever those who draw near to God through Him, since He always lives to make intercession for them" (Heb 7:25). Jesus' divine work of redemption in a believer's heart begins at the time of conversion, but it does not end until that saint is in heaven, glorified and made as righteous as God is righteous, because he possesses the full righteousness of Christ. That is guaranteed by the heavenly high priestly work of our Lord and by the earthly indwelling Holy **Spirit,** which also make secure the divine adoption and heavenly destiny of every believer.

If it were not for the sustaining power of the Spirit within us and Christ's continual mediation for us as High Priest (Heb 7:25–26), our remaining humanness would have immediately engulfed us again in sin the moment after we were justified. If for an instant Christ and the Holy Spirit were to stop their sustaining intercession for us, we would, in that instant, fall back into our sinful, damnable state of separation from God.

If such a falling away could happen, faith in Christ would give us only temporary spiritual life, subject at any moment to loss. But Jesus offers no life but eternal life, which, by definition, cannot be lost. To those who believe, Jesus said, "I give eternal life, ... and they shall never perish; and no one shall snatch them out of My hand" (John 10:28; cf. 17:2–3; Acts 13:48). To have faith in Jesus Christ and to have eternal life are scripturally synonymous.

Were it not for the sustaining and intercessory work of the Son and the Spirit on behalf of believers, Satan and his false teachers could easily deceive God's elect (see Matt 24:24) and could undermine the completion of their salvation. But if such a thing were possible, God's election would be meaningless. Satan knows that believers would be helpless apart from the sustaining work of the Son and the Spirit, and in his arrogant pride he vainly wars against those two divine persons of the Godhead. He knows that if somehow he could interrupt that divine protection, once-saved souls would fall from grace and again belong to him. But the never-ending work of Christ and the Holy Spirit make that impossible.

And He who searches the hearts knows what the mind of the Spirit is, Paul continues. He refers to God the Father, **who searches the hearts** of men.

In the process of selecting a successor to King Saul, the Lord told Samuel, "God sees not as man sees, for man looks at the outward appearance, but the Lord looks at the heart" (1 Sam 16:7). At the dedication of the Temple, Solomon prayed, "Hear Thou in heaven

Thy dwelling place, and forgive and act and render to each according to all his ways, whose heart Thou knowest, for Thou alone dost know the hearts of all the sons of men" (1 Kgs 8:39; cf. 1 Chron 28:9; Ps 139:1–2; Prov 15:11). When they were choosing between Joseph Barsabbas and Matthias as a successor for Judas, the eleven apostles prayed, "Thou, Lord, who knowest the hearts of all men, show which one of these two Thou hast chosen" (Acts 1:24; cf. 1 Cor 4:5; Heb 4:13).

If the Father knows the hearts of men, how much more does He know **the mind of the Spirit.** The Father understands exactly what the **Spirit** is thinking **because He intercedes for the saints according to the will of God.** Because the Spirit's will and the Father's will are identical, and because God is one, Paul's statement seems unnecessary. But he is pointing up the truth in order to give encouragement to believers. Because the three persons of the Godhead have always been one in essence and will, the very idea of communication among them seems superfluous to us. It is a great mystery to our finite minds, but it is a divine reality that God expects His children to acknowledge by faith.

In this passage Paul emphasizes the divine intercession that is necessary for the preservation of believers to their eternal hope. We can no more fathom that marvelous truth than we can fathom any other aspect of God's plan of redemption. But we know that, were not Christ and the Holy Spirit continually on guard in our behalf, our inheritance in heaven would be reserved for us in vain.

06

THE ULTIMATE SECURITY—PART 1
THE INFALLIBLE GUARANTEE
OF GLORY

ROMANS 8:28

A nd we know that God causes all things to work together for good to those who love God, to those who are called according to His purpose. (8:28)

For Christians, this verse contains perhaps the most glorious promise in Scripture. It is breathtaking in its magnitude, encompassing absolutely *everything* that pertains to a believer's life. This magnificent promise consists of four elements that continue Paul's teaching about the believer's security in the Holy Spirit: its certainty, its extent, its recipients, and its source.

THE CERTAINTY OF SECURITY

And we know ... (8:28*a*)

In the context of the truths that follow in Romans 8, these three simple words express the Christian's absolute certainty of eternal security in the Holy Spirit. Paul is not expressing his personal intuitions or opinions but is setting forth the inerrant truth of God's Word. It is not Paul the man, but Paul the apostle and channel of God's revelation who continues to declare the truth he has received from the Holy Spirit. He therefore asserts with God's own authority that, as believers in Jesus Christ, **we know** beyond all doubt that every aspect of our lives is in God's hands and will be divinely used by the Lord not only to manifest His own glory but also to work out our own ultimate blessing.

The phrase **we know** here carries the meaning of know. Tragically, many Christians throughout the history of the church, including many in our own day, refuse to believe that God guarantees the believer's eternal security. Such denial is tied to the belief that salvation is a cooperative effort between men and God, and although God will not fail on His side, man might—thus the sense of insecurity. Belief in salvation by a sovereign God alone, however, leads to the confidence that salvation is secure, because God, who alone is responsible, cannot fail. Beyond that theological consideration Paul is saying that the truth of eternal security is clearly revealed by God to us, so that all believers *are able* with certainty to **know** the comfort and hope of that reality if they simply take God at His word. God's child need never fear being cast out of his heavenly Father's house or fear losing his citizenship in His eternal kingdom of righteousness.

THE EXTENT OF SECURITY

that God causes all things to work together for good ... (8:28*b*)

The extent of the believer's security is as limitless as its certainty is absolute. As with every other element of the believer's security, **God** is the Guarantor. It is He who **causes** everything in the believer's life to eventuate in blessing.

Paul emphasizes that **God** Himself brings about the good that comes to His people. This magnificent promise does not operate through impersonal statements, but requires divine action to fulfill. God's decree of security is actually carried out by the direct, personal, and gracious work of His divine Son and His Holy Spirit. "Hence, also, [Christ] is able to save forever those who draw near to God through Him, since He always lives to make intercession for them" (Heb 7:25). And as Paul has just proclaimed, "The Spirit Himself intercedes for us with groanings too deep for words; and He who searches the hearts knows what the mind of the Spirit is, because He intercedes for the saints according to the will of God" (Rom 8:26–27).

All things is utterly comprehensive, having no qualifications or limits. Neither this verse nor its context allows for restrictions or conditions. **All things** is inclusive in the fullest possible sense. Nothing existing or occurring in heaven or on earth "shall be able to separate us from the love of God, which is in Christ Jesus" (8:39).

Paul is not saying that God prevents His children from experiencing **things** that can harm them. He is rather attesting that the Lord takes all that He allows to happen to His beloved children, even the worst things, and turns those things ultimately into blessings.

Paul teaches the same basic truth in several of his other letters. "So then let no one boast in men," he admonishes the Corinthian believers. "For all things belong to you, whether Paul or Apollos or Cephas or the world or life or death or things present or things to come; all things belong to you" (1 Cor 3:21–22). Perhaps a year later he assured them in another letter: "For all things are for your sakes, that the grace which is spreading to more and more people may cause the giving of thanks to abound to the glory of God" (2 Cor 4:15). Later in Romans 8 Paul asks rhetorically, "He who did not spare His own Son, but delivered Him up for us all, how will He not also with Him freely give us all things?" (v. 32).

No matter what our situation, our suffering, our persecution, our sinful failure, our pain, our lack of faith—in those things, as well as in **all** other **things,** our heavenly Father will work to produce our ultimate victory and blessing. The corollary of that truth is that nothing can ultimately work against us. Any temporary harm we suffer will be used by God for our benefit (see 2 Cor 12:7–10). As will be discussed below, **all things** includes circumstances and events that are good and beneficial in themselves as well as those that are in themselves evil and harmful.

To work together translates *sunergeō*, from which is derived the English term *synergism*, the working together of various elements to produce an effect greater than, and often completely different from, the sum of each element acting separately. In the physical world the right combination of otherwise harmful chemicals can produce substances that are extremely beneficial. For example, ordinary table salt is composed of two poisons, sodium and chlorine.

Contrary to what the King James rendering seems to suggest, it is not that things in themselves work together to produce good. As Paul has made clear earlier in the verse, it is God's providential power and will, not a natural synergism of circumstances and events in our lives, that causes them **to work together for good.** David testified to that marvelous truth when he exulted, "All the paths of the Lord are lovingkindness and truth to those who keep His covenant and His testimonies" (Ps 25:10). No matter what road we are on or path we take, the Lord will turn it into a way of lovingkindness and truth.

Paul likely has in mind our **good** during this present life as well as ultimately in the life to come. No matter what happens in our lives as His children, the providence of God uses it for our temporal as well as our eternal benefit, sometimes by saving us from tragedies and sometimes by sending us through them in order to draw us closer to Him.

After delivering the Israelites from Egyptian bondage, God continually provided for their well-being as they faced the harsh obstacles of the Sinai desert. As Moses proclaimed the law to Israel, he reminded the people: "[God] led you through the great and terrible wilderness, with its fiery serpents and scorpions and thirsty ground where there was no water; He brought water for you out of the rock of flint. In the wilderness He fed you manna which your fathers did not know, that He might humble you and that He might test you, to do good for you in the end" (Deut 8:15–16). The Lord did not lead His people through forty years of difficulty and hardship to bring them evil but to bring them **good,** the good that sometimes must come by way of divine discipline and refining.

It is clear from that illustration, as well as from countless others in Scripture, that God often delays the temporal as well as the ultimate **good** that He promises. Jeremiah declared, "Thus says the Lord God of Israel, 'Like these good figs, so I will regard as good the captives of Judah, whom I have sent out of this place into the land of the Chaldeans. For I will set My eyes on them for good, and I will bring them again to this land; and I will build them up and not overthrow them, and I will plant them and not pluck them up. And I will give them a heart to know Me, for I am the Lord; and they will be My people, and I will be their God, for they will return to Me with their whole heart'"

(Jer 24:5–7). In His sovereign graciousness, the Lord used the painful and frustrating captivities of Israel and Judah to refine His people, and by human reckoning, the process was slow and arduous.

"Therefore we do not lose heart," Paul counseled the Corinthian believers, "but though our outer man is decaying, yet our inner man is being renewed day by day. For momentary, light affliction is producing for us an eternal weight of glory far beyond all comparison" (2 Cor 4:16–17). Even when our outward circumstances are dire—perhaps *especially* when they are dire and seemingly hopeless from our perspective—God is purifying and renewing our redeemed inner beings in preparation for glorification, the ultimate **good.**

First of all, God causes righteous things to work for our **good.** By far the most significant and best of good things are God's own attributes. God's *power* supports us in our troubles and strengthens our spiritual life. In his final blessing of the children of Israel, Moses testified, "The eternal God is a dwelling place, and underneath are the everlasting arms" (Deut 33:27). In His parting words to the apostles, Jesus promised, "You shall receive power when the Holy Spirit has come upon you; and you shall be My witnesses both in Jerusalem, and in all Judea and Samaria, and even to the remotest part of the earth" (Acts 1:8).

In order to demonstrate our utter dependence upon God, His power working through us is actually "perfected in weakness. Most gladly, therefore," Paul testified, "I will rather boast about my weaknesses, that the power of Christ may dwell in me" (2 Cor 12:9).

God's *wisdom* provides for our **good.** The most direct way is by sharing His wisdom with us. Paul prayed that the Lord would give the Ephesian believers "a spirit of wisdom and of revelation in the knowledge of Him" (Eph 1:17). He made similar requests on behalf of the Colossians: "We have not ceased to pray for you and to ask that you may be filled with the knowledge of His will in all spiritual wisdom and understanding" (Col 1:9), and later, "Let the word of Christ richly dwell within you, with all wisdom teaching and admonishing one another with psalms and hymns and spiritual songs, singing with thankfulness in your hearts to God" (3:16).

Almost by definition, God's *goodness* works to the **good** of His children. "Do you think lightly of the riches of His kindness and forbearance and patience," Paul reminds us, "not knowing that the kindness of God leads you to repentance?" (Rom 2:4).

God's *faithfulness* works for our **good.** Even when His children are unfaithful to Him, their heavenly Father remains faithful to them. "I will heal their apostasy, I will love them freely, for My anger has turned away from them" (Hos 14:4). Micah rejoiced in the Lord, exulting, "Who is a God like Thee, who pardons iniquity and passes over the rebellious act of the remnant of His possession? He does not retain His anger forever, because He delights in unchanging love" (Mic 7:18). When a child of God is in need, the Lord promises, "He will call upon Me, and I will answer him; I will be with him in trouble; I will rescue him, and honor him" (Ps 91:15). "My God shall supply all your needs," Paul assures us, "according to His riches in glory in Christ Jesus" (Phil 4:19).

God's *Word* is for our **good.** "And now I commend you to God and to the word of His grace, which is able to build you up and to give you the inheritance among all those who are sanctified" (Acts 20:32). Every good thing we receive from God's hand "is sanctified by means of the word of God and prayer" (1 Tim 4:5). The more we see sin through the eyes of Scripture, which is to see it through God's own eyes, the more we abhor it.

In addition to His attributes, God's *holy angels* work for the **good** of those who belong to Him. "Are they not all ministering spirits," the writer of Hebrews asks rhetorically about the angels, "sent out to render service for the sake of those who will inherit salvation?" (Heb 1:14).

God's *children* themselves are ministers of His **good** to each other. In the opening of his letter to Rome, Paul humbly assured his readers that he longed to visit them not only to minister *to* them but to be ministered to *by* them, "that is, that I may be encouraged together with you while among you, each of us by the other's faith, both yours and mine"

(Rom 1:12). To the Corinthian believers the apostle described himself and Timothy as "workers with you for your joy" (2 Cor 1:24; cf. v. 1). It is both the obligation and the joy of Christians "to stimulate one another to love and good deeds" (Heb 10:24).

Although the truth is often difficult to recognize and accept, the Lord causes even *evil* things to work for our **good.** It is these less obvious and less pleasant channels of God's blessing that Paul here seems to be emphasizing—those things among the "all things" that are in themselves anything but good. Many of the things that we do and that happen to us are either outright evil or, at best, are worthless. Yet in His infinite wisdom and omnipotence, our heavenly Father will turn even the worst of such things to our ultimate **good.**

As mentioned above, God used His people's slavery in Egypt and their trials in the wilderness not only to demonstrate His power against their enemies on their behalf but to refine and purify His people before they took possession of the Promised Land. Although the afflictions and hardships in the Sinai desert hardened the hearts of most of the people and made them rebellious, God intended those trials to be for their blessing.

When Daniel was threatened with death for refusing to obey King Darius's ban on worshiping any god but the king, the monarch reluctantly had the prophet thrown into the den of lions. When it became evident that the lions would not harm him, Daniel testified to Darius, "'O king, live forever! My God sent His angel and shut the lions' mouths, and they have not harmed me, inasmuch as I was found innocent before Him; and also toward you, O king, I have committed no crime." Then the king was very pleased and gave orders for Daniel to be taken up out of the den. So Daniel was taken up out of the den, and no injury whatever was found on him, because he had trusted in his God" (Dan 6:21–23). The suffering and martyrdom of many of His saints, however, is clear evidence that God does not always choose to bless faithfulness by deliverance from harm.

The evil things that God uses for the **good** of His people may be divided into three categories: suffering, temptation, and sin.

God uses the evil of suffering as a means of bringing **good** *to His people.* Sometimes the suffering comes as the price of faithfulness to God. At other times it is simply the common pain, hardship, disease, and conflicts that are the lot of all mankind because of sin's corruption of the world. At still other times the suffering comes by God's permission, and not always as punishment or discipline. The godly Naomi lamented, "Call me Mara, for the Almighty has dealt very bitterly with me" (Ruth 1:20). After the bewildering afflictions with which God allowed him to be tormented by Satan, Job responded in simple trust: "The Lord gave and the Lord has taken away. Blessed be the name of the Lord" (Job 1:21).

Often, of course, suffering *does* come as divine chastisement for sin. God promised Judah that, despite the rebellion and idolatry that caused her captivity, "I will regard as good the captives of Judah, whom I have sent out of this place into the land of the Chaldeans" (Jer 24:5). God chastened certain members of the Corinthian church because of their flagrant and unrepentant sins, causing some to become sick and others to die (1 Cor 11:29–30). We are not told what good God brought to those sinful believers themselves. Perhaps it was simply His means of preventing them from falling into worse sin. It is likely that He worked good for the rest of the Corinthian church as He had done in the instance of Ananias and Sapphira, whose severe discipline was a purifying force, causing "great fear [to come] upon the whole church, and upon all who heard of these things" (Acts 5:11).

Regardless of what our adversities might be or how they might come, James admonishes us to "consider it all joy, my brethren, when You encounter various trials, knowing that the testing of your faith produces endurance" (Jas 1:2–3). Trials that come directly because of our relationship to Christ should be especially welcomed, Peter says, "that the proof of your faith, being more precious than gold which is perishable, even though tested by fire, may be found to result in praise and glory and honor at the revelation of Jesus Christ" (1 Pet 1:7).

Joseph is a classic Old Testament example of God's using unjust suffering to bring great **good,** not only to the sufferer himself but to all of his family, who constituted God's chosen people. If he had never been sold into slavery and cast into prison, he would not have had the opportunity to interpret Pharaoh's dream and rise to a position of great prominence, from which he could be used to save Egypt and his own people from starvation. Understanding that marvelous truth, Joseph told his fearful brothers, "And as for you, you meant evil against me, but God meant it for good in order to bring about this present result, to preserve many people alive" (Gen 50:20).

King Manasseh of Judah brought foreign conquest and great suffering upon himself and his nation because of his sinfulness. But "when he was in distress, he entreated the Lord his God and humbled himself greatly before the God of his fathers. When he prayed to Him, He was moved by his entreaty and heard his supplication, and brought him again to Jerusalem to his kingdom. Then Manasseh knew that the Lord was God" (2 Chron 33:12–13).

Although Job never lost faith in God, his incessant afflictions eventually caused him to question the Lord's ways. After a severe rebuke by God, however, Job confessed, "I have heard of Thee by the hearing of the ear; but now my eye sees Thee; therefore I retract, and I repent in dust and ashes" (Job 42:5–6).

An enemy aggressively afflicted pain on the apostle Paul. Very likely he was the leader of Corinthian hostility toward Paul. Paul knew that, although this person belonged to Satan's domain, his activity against the apostle was permitted by God to keep him (Paul) from exalting himself because of his visions and revelations (2 Cor 12:6–7). Nevertheless, Paul pleaded earnestly three times that he might be delivered from the man's attacks. The Lord responded by telling His faithful servant, "My grace is sufficient for you, for power is perfected in weakness." That explanation was sufficient for Paul, who said submissively, "Most gladly, therefore, I will rather boast about my weaknesses, that the power of Christ may dwell in me. Therefore I am well content with weaknesses, with insults, with distresses, with persecutions, with difficulties, for Christ's sake; for when I am weak, then I am strong" (2 Cor 12:9–10). Instead of turning down the trouble, God turned up the sufficient grace, so that Paul could endure the situation gladly and be humbled by it at the same time.

Through suffering of all kinds and for all reasons, we can learn kindness, sympathy, humility, compassion, patience, and gentleness. Most importantly, God can use suffering as He can use few other things to bring us closer to Himself. "And after you have suffered for a little while," Peter reassures us, "the God of all grace, who called you to His eternal glory in Christ, will Himself perfect, confirm, strengthen and establish you"

(1 Pet 5:10). The Puritan Thomas Watson observed, "A sick-bed often teaches more than a sermon" (*A Divine Cordial* [Grand Rapids: Baker, 1981], p. 20).

Suffering can also teach us to hate sin. We already hate sin to some degree, because it is the direct or indirect cause of all suffering. But personally suffering at the hands of evil men will teach us more about the wickedness of sin. Martin Luther said that he could never understand the imprecatory psalms until he himself was persecuted viciously. He could not understand why the godly David could call down God's vengeance on his enemies until he himself [Luther] had been tormented by enemies of the gospel.

We also come to hate sin when we see its destruction of others, especially its harm to those we love. Jesus groaned in agony at Lazarus's tomb, but not because He despaired for His deceased friend, because He would momentarily remedy that. He was angry and saddened because of the grief that sin and its greatest consequence, death, brought to the loved ones of Lazarus (see John 11:33). He also realized that such agony is multiplied a million times over every day throughout the world.

Suffering helps us see and hate our own sin. Sometimes it is only when we are mistreated, unfairly accused, or are debilitated by illness, financial disaster, or some other form of hardship that we come face-to-face with our temper, our self-satisfaction, or our indifference to other people and even to God. By helping us see and hate our sin, suffering is also used by God to drive it out and purify us. "When He has tried me," Job said, "I shall come forth as gold" (Job 23:10). In the last days, "'It will come about in all the land,' declares the Lord, 'that two parts in it will be cut off and perish; but the third will be left in it. And I will bring the third part through the fire, refine them as silver is refined, and test them as gold is tested. They will call on My name, and I will answer them; I will say, "They are My people," and they will say, "The Lord is my God"'" (Zech 13:8–9). Through that final and unparalleled period of suffering, the Lord will refine and restore to Himself a remnant of His ancient people Israel.

Suffering divine discipline confirms that we are indeed God's children. The writer of Hebrews reminds us that "those whom the Lord loves He disciplines, and He scourges every son whom He receives. It is for discipline that you endure; God deals with you as with sons; for what son is there whom his father does not discipline? But if you are without discipline, of which all have become partakers, then you are illegitimate children and not sons" (Heb 12:6–8; cf. Job 5:17).

As the writer of Hebrews notes, wise human parents discipline their children for the children's own welfare. Even secular psychologists and counselors have come to recognize that a child who is overindulged in what he wants, but given no bounds and held to no standards by his parents, realizes innately that he is not loved.

Three times the writer of Psalm 119 acknowledged that the Lord used suffering to strengthen his spiritual life: "Before I was afflicted I went astray, but now I keep Thy word" (v. 67); "It is good for me that I was afflicted, that I may learn Thy statutes" (v. 71); and, "I know, O Lord, that Thy judgments are righteous, and that in faithfulness Thou hast afflicted me" (v. 75).

Suffering is designed by God to help us identify to a limited extent with Christ's suffering on our behalf and to conform us to Him. It is for that reason that Paul prayed to "know Him, and the power of His resurrection and the fellowship of His sufferings, being conformed to His death" (Phil 3:10), and that he boasted, "I bear on my body the brandmarks of Jesus" (Gal 6:17). When we willingly submit it to our heavenly Father, suffering can be used by Him to mold us more perfectly into the divine likeness of our Lord and Savior.

God uses the evil of temptation as a means of bringing **good** *to His people.* Just as suffering is not good in itself, neither, of course, is temptation. But, as is the case with suffering, the Lord is able to use temptation for our benefit.

Temptation should drive us to our knees in prayer and cause us to ask God for strength to resist. When an animal sees a predator, he runs or flies as fast as he can to a place of safety. That should be the Christian's response whenever he is confronted by temptation.

Temptation causes the godly believer to flee to the Lord for protection.

Whether Satan approaches us as a roaring lion or as an angel of light, if we are well taught in God's Word we can recognize his evil enticements for what they are. That is why the psalmist proclaimed, "Thy word I have treasured in my heart, that I may not sin against Thee" (Ps 119:11).

God can also cause temptation to work for our good by using it to devastate spiritual pride. When we struggle with temptation, we know that, in ourselves, we are still subject to the allurements and defilements of sin. And when we try to resist it in our own power, we quickly discover how powerless against it we are in ourselves.

In His incarnation, even Jesus did not resist Satan's temptation in His humanness but in every instance confronted the tempter with the Word of God (Matt 4:1–10; Luke 4:1–12). Our response to Satan's enticements should be the same as our Lord's while He was on earth. Christ's experience with temptation not only provides us with a divine example but provided Christ with human experience—in light of which the writer of Hebrews could declare, "For we do not have a high priest who cannot sympathize with our weaknesses, but one who has been tempted in all things as we are, yet without sin" (Heb 4:15).

Finally, temptation should strengthen the believer's desire for heaven, where he will be forever beyond sin's allurement, power, and presence. When in frustration we cry out with Paul, "Who will set me free from the body of this death?" we can also proclaim with him, "Thanks be to God through Jesus Christ our Lord! So then, on the one hand I myself with my mind am serving the law of God, but on the other, with my flesh the law of sin" (Rom 7:24–25). We can also confess with the apostle that, although we are willing to remain on earth to fulfill the Lord's ministry through us, our great longing is to be with Him (Phil 1:21–24).

God uses the evil of sin as a means of bringing good *to His children.* That would have to be true if Paul's statement about "all things" is taken at face value. Even more than suffering and temptation, sin is not good in itself, because it is the antithesis of good. Yet, in God's infinite wisdom and power, it is most remarkable of all that He turns sin to our good.

It is of great importance, of course, to recognize that God does not use sin for good in the sense of its being an instrument of His righteousness. That would be the most obvious of self-contradictions. The Lord uses sin to bring good to His children by overruling it, canceling its normal evil consequences and miraculously substituting His benefits.

Because it is often easier for us to recognize the reality and the wickedness of sin in others than in ourselves, God can cause the sins of other people to work for our good. If we are seeking to live a godly life in Christ, seeing a sin in others will make us hate and avoid it more. A spirit of judgmental self-righteousness, of course, will have the opposite effect, leading us into the snare about which Paul has already warned: "In that you judge another, you condemn yourself; for you who judge practice the same things. And we know that the judgment of God rightly falls upon those who practice such things. And do you suppose this, O man, when you pass judgment upon those who practice such things and do the same yourself, that you will escape the judgment of God?" (Rom 2:1–3; cf. Matt 7:1–2).

God can even cause our own sins to work for our good. A believer's sins are just as evil as those of unbelievers. But the ultimate consequence of a believer's sin is vastly different, because the penalty for *all* his sins—past, present, and future—has been paid in full by his Savior. Although the foundational truth of Romans 8 is that, by God's unspeakable grace, a Christian is forever preserved from sin's *ultimate* consequence, which is eternal condemnation (v. 1), a Christian is still subject to the immediate, temporal consequences of sins he commits, as well as to many continuing consequences of sins committed before salvation. As noted several times above, the sinning believer is not spared God's chastisement but is assured of it as a remedial tool for producing holiness (Heb 12:10). That is the supreme good for which God causes our sin to work.

God also causes our own sin to work for our good by leading us to despise the sin and to desire His holiness. When we fall into sin, our spiritual weakness becomes evident and we are driven humbly to seek God's forgiveness and restoration. Evil as it is, sin can bring us good by stripping us of our pride and self-assurance.

The supreme illustration of God's turning "all things," even the most evil of things, to the good of His children is seen in the sacrificial death of His own Son. In the crucifixion of Jesus Christ, God took the most absolute evil that Satan could devise and turned it into the greatest conceivable blessing.

THE RECIPIENTS OF SECURITY

to those who love God, to those who are called … (8:28c)

The only qualification in the marvelous promise of this verse has to do with the recipients. It is solely for His children that God promises to work everything for good. **Those who love God** and **those who are called** are two of the many titles or descriptions the New Testament uses of Christians. From the human perspective we are **those who love God,** whereas from God's perspective we are **those who are called.**

THE RECIPIENTS OF SECURITY LOVE GOD
to those who love God ...

First, Paul describes the recipients of eternal security as **those who love God.** Nothing more characterizes the true believer than genuine **love** for **God.** Redeemed people **love** the gracious **God** who has saved them. Because of their depraved and sinful natures, the unredeemed hate God, regardless of any arguments they may have to the contrary. When God made His covenant with Israel through Moses, He made the distinction clear between those who love Him and those who hate Him. In the Ten Commandments the Lord told His people, "You shall not worship [idols] or serve them; for I, the Lord your God, am a jealous God, visiting the iniquity of the fathers on the children, on the third and the fourth generations of those who hate Me, but showing lovingkindness to thousands, to those who love Me and keep My commandments" (Exod 20:5–6; cf. Deut 7:9–10; Neh 1:4–5; Pss 69:36; 97:10). In God's sight, there are only two categories of human beings, those who hate Him and those who love Him. Jesus was referring to that truth when He said, "He who is not with Me is against Me" (Matt 12:30).

Even during the time of the Mosaic covenant, when God was dealing with His chosen people Israel in a unique way, any person, even a Gentile, who trusted in Him was accepted by Him and was characterized by love for the Lord. God's redeemed included "also the foreigners who join themselves to the Lord, to minister to Him, and to love the name of the Lord, to be His servants, every one who keeps from profaning the sabbath, and holds fast My covenant" (Isa 56:6).

The New Testament is equally clear that those who belong to God love Him. "Just as it is written," Paul reminded the Corinthians, "Things which eye has not seen and ear has not heard, and which have not entered the heart of man, all that God has prepared for those who love Him'" (1 Cor 2:9; cf. Isa 64:4). Later in that letter he declared, "If anyone loves God, he is known by Him" (1 Cor 8:3).

James says that those who love God, that is, believers, are promised the Lord's eternal crown of life (Jas 1:12). Paul refers to Christians as "those who love our Lord Jesus Christ with a love incorruptible" (Eph 6:24).

Saving faith involves much more than simply acknowledging God. Even the demons fearfully believe that God is one and is all-powerful (Jas 2:19). True faith involves the surrendering of one's sinful self to God for forgiveness and receiving Jesus Christ as Lord and Savior. And the first mark of saving faith is love for God. True salvation produces lovers of God, because "the love of God has been poured out within our hearts through the Holy Spirit who was given to us" (Rom 5:5). It is not by accident that Paul lists love as the first fruit of the Spirit (Gal 5:22).

Love for God is closely related to forgiveness, because the redeemed believer cannot help being grateful for God's gracious forgiveness. When the sinful woman, doubtlessly a prostitute, washed and anointed Jesus' feet in the Pharisee's house, the Lord explained to His resentful host that she expressed great love because she had been forgiven great sins (Luke 7:47).

Love for God is also related to obedience. "And why do you call Me, 'Lord, Lord,' " Jesus said, "and do not do what I say?" (Luke 6:46). The persistently disobedient heart is an unbelieving and unloving heart. Because "the love of Christ controls us" (2 Cor 5:14), His Word will also control us. "You are My friends," Jesus said, "if you do what I command you" (John 15:14). In context, it is clear that Jesus uses the term *friend* as a synonym for a true disciple (see vv. 8–17).

Obviously we do not love Christ as fully as we ought because we are still imperfect and are contaminated by the sinful remnants of the old self. It is for that reason Paul told the Philippians, "And this I pray, that your love may abound still more and more in real knowledge and all discernment" (Phil 1:9). Their love for Christ was genuine, but it was not yet perfect.

Genuine love for God has many facets and manifestations. First, godly love longs for personal communion with the Lord. It was that desire which led the psalmists to proclaim, "As the deer pants for the water brooks, so my soul pants for Thee, O God. My soul thirsts for God, for the living God; when shall I come and appear before God?" (Ps 42:1–2), and "Whom have I in heaven but Thee? And besides Thee, I desire nothing on earth" (Ps 73:25).

David prayed, "O God, Thou art my God; I shall seek Thee earnestly; my soul thirsts for Thee, my flesh yearns for Thee, in a dry and weary land where there is no water. Thus I have beheld Thee in the sanctuary, to see Thy power and Thy glory. Because Thy lovingkindness is better than life, my lips will praise Thee" (Ps 63:1–3). Speaking for all faithful believers, the sons of Korah exulted, "My soul longed and even yearned for the courts of the Lord; my heart and my flesh sing for joy to the living God. The bird also has found a house, and the swallow a nest for herself, where she may lay her young, even Thine altars, O Lord of hosts, my King and my God. How blessed are those who dwell in Thy house! They are ever praising Thee" (Ps 84:2–4).

Second, genuine love for God trusts in His power to protect His own. David admonished fellow believers: "O love the Lord, all you His godly ones! The Lord preserves the faithful" (Ps 31:23).

Third, genuine love for God is characterized by peace that only He can impart. "Those who love Thy law have great peace, and nothing causes them to stumble" (Ps 119:165). As believers, we have a divine and secure peace that the world cannot give, possess, understand, or take away (John 14:27; 16:33; Phil 4:7).

Fourth, genuine love for God is sensitive to His will and His honor. When God is blasphemed, repudiated, or in any way dishonored, His faithful children suffer pain on His behalf. David so identified himself with the Lord that he could say, "Zeal for Thy house has consumed me, and the reproaches of those who reproach Thee have fallen on me" (Ps 69:9).

Fifth, genuine love for God loves the things that God loves, and we know what He loves through the revelation of His Word. Throughout Psalm 119 the writer expresses love for God's law, God's ways, God's standards, and all else that is God's. "The law of Thy mouth is better to me Than thousands of gold and silver pieces" (v. 72); "O how I love Thy law! It is my meditation all the day" (v. 97); and "How sweet are Thy words to my taste! Yes, sweeter than honey to my mouth!" (v. 103). David testified: "I will bow down toward Thy holy temple, and give thanks to Thy name for Thy lovingkindness and Thy truth; for Thou hast magnified Thy word according to all Thy name" (Ps 138:2).

Sixth, genuine love for God loves the people God loves. John repeatedly and unequivocally asserts that a person who does not love God's children does not love God and does not belong to God. "We know that we have passed out of death into life," the apostle says, "because we love the brethren. He who does not love abides in death" (1 John 3:14). "Beloved, let us love one another, for love is from God; and everyone who loves is born of God and knows God. The one who does not love does not know God, for God is love" (4:7–8). In the strongest possible language, John declares that "if someone says, 'I love God,' and hates his brother, he is a liar; for the one who does not love his brother whom he has seen, cannot love God whom he has not seen. And this commandment we have from Him, that the one who loves God should love his brother also" (4:20–21). In the next chapter he declares just as firmly that "whoever loves the Father loves the child born of Him. By this we know that we love the children of God, when we love God and observe His commandments" (1 John 5:1–2).

Seventh, genuine love for God hates what God hates. Godly love cannot tolerate evil. The loving Christian grieves over sin, first of all for sin in his own life but also for sin in the lives of others, especially in the lives of fellow believers. When the cock's crow reminded Peter of his Lord's prediction, he wept bitterly over his denial of Christ, which he had just made for the third time (Matt 26:75).

On the other hand, to love the world and the things of the world is to love what God hates, and John therefore solemnly warns, "If anyone loves the world, the love of the Father is not in him" (1 John 2:15).

Eighth, genuine love for God longs for Christ's return. Paul rejoiced in the knowledge that "in the future there is laid up for me the crown of righteousness, which the Lord, the righteous Judge, will award to me on that day; and not only to me, but also to all who have loved His appearing" (2 Tim 4:8).

Ninth and finally, the overarching mark of genuine love for God is obedience. "He who has My commandments and keeps them," Jesus said, "he it is who loves Me; and he who loves Me shall be loved by My Father, and I will love him, and will disclose Myself to him" (John 14:21). As noted above in the citation of 1 John 5:1–2, obedience to God is inextricably tied both to love for God and love for fellow believers.

Although we are commanded to love God and fellow believers, that love does not and cannot originate with us. Godly love is God-given. "Love is from God," John explains, and therefore it is "not that we loved God, but that He loved us and sent His Son to be the propitiation for our sins" (1 John 4:7, 10). We are able to love only because God has first loved us (v. 19).

THE RECIPIENTS OF SECURITY ARE CALLED
to those who are called …

Second, Paul describes the recipients of eternal security as **those who are called.** Just as our love originates with God, so does our calling into His heavenly family. In every way, the initiative and provision for salvation are God's. In their fallen, sinful state, men are able only to hate God, because, regardless of what they may think, they are His enemies (Rom 5:10) and children of His wrath (Eph 2:3).

When Jesus said that "many are called, but few are chosen" (Matt 22:14), He was referring to the gospel's external call to all men to believe in Him. In the history of the church nothing is more obvious than the fact that many, perhaps most, people who receive this call do not accept it.

But in the epistles, the terms *called* and *calling* are used in a different sense, referring to the sovereign, regenerating work of God in a believer's heart that brings him to new life in Christ. Paul explains the meaning of **those who are called** in the following two verses (29–30), where he speaks of what theologians often refer to as God's effectual call. In this sense, *all* **those who are called** are chosen and redeemed by God and are ultimately glorified. They are securely predestined by God to be His children and to be conformed to the image of His Son.

Believers have never been **called** on the basis of their works or for their own purposes. As Hebrews 11 makes clear, faith in God has always been the only way of redemption. Believers are not saved on the basis of who they are or what they have done but solely on the basis of who God is and what He has done. We are redeemed "according to His own purpose and grace which was granted us in Christ Jesus from all eternity" (2 Tim 1:9). Because it operates completely according to God's will and by His power, the gospel never fails to accomplish and secure its work of salvation in those who believe (1 Thess 2:13).

Later in Romans Paul uses Jacob and Esau to illustrate God's effectual call, which is also a sovereign call. "For though the twins were not yet born," he says, "and had not done anything good or bad, in order that God's purpose according to His choice might stand, not because of works, but because of Him who calls, it was said to her, 'The older will serve the younger.' Just as it is written, 'Jacob I loved, but Esau I hated' " (Rom 9:11–13).

Although human faith is imperative for salvation, God's gracious initiation of salvation is even more imperative. Jesus declared categorically, "No one can come to Me, unless it has been granted him from the Father" (John 6:65). God's choice not only precedes man's choice but makes man's choice possible and effective.

Paul not only was called by Christ to salvation (see Acts 9) but was also "called as an apostle of Jesus Christ by the will of God" (1 Cor 1:1). He describes himself as being "laid hold of by Christ Jesus" (Phil 3:12). Paul addressed believers at Corinth as "those who have been sanctified in Christ Jesus, saints by calling" (1 Cor 1:2), and later refers to all Christians as "those who are the called, both Jews and Greeks" (v. 24). All believers, without exception, are called by God, "having been predestined according to His purpose who works all things after the counsel of His will" (Eph 1:11).

In its primary sense, God's call is once and for all, but in a secondary sense it continues until the believer is finally glorified. Although he acknowledged his permanent call both as a believer and as an apostle, Paul could yet say, "I press on toward the goal for the prize of the upward call of God in Christ Jesus" (Phil 3:14).

As already noted, although salvation is by God's initiative and power, it is never accomplished apart from faith. It is therefore impossible, as some teach, that a person can be saved and never know it. No person is saved apart from conscious and willful acceptance of Christ. "If you confess with your mouth Jesus as Lord, and believe in your heart that God raised Him from the dead," Paul says, "you shall be saved; for with the heart man believes, resulting in righteousness, and with the mouth he confesses, resulting in salvation" (Rom 10:9–10). It is possible, of course, for a weak, unlearned, or sinful Christian to have later doubts about his salvation. But a person cannot come to Christ without knowing it.

As Paul explains a few verses later, God also uses human agents in making effective His call to salvation. "How then shall they call upon Him in whom they have not believed? And how shall they believe in Him whom they have not heard? And how shall they hear without a preacher?" (Rom 10:14).

It is through the content of His Word, specifically the truth of the gospel message, and through the power of His Holy Spirit that God brings men to Himself. Peter succinctly states the first of those two principles: "You have been born again not of seed which is perishable but imperishable, that is, through the living and abiding word of God" (1 Pet 1:23). Paul states the second principle in these words: "For by one Spirit we were all baptized into one body, whether Jews or Greeks, whether slaves or free, and we were all made to drink of one Spirit" (1 Cor 12:13; cf. John 16:8).

THE SOURCE OF SECURITY

according to His purpose. (8:28*d*)

At the end of verse 28, Paul states the source of the believer's security in Christ. God causes all things to work together for the good of His children because that is **according to His** divine **purpose.** Although the Greek text does not contain the term for **His,** that meaning is clearly implied in the context and is reflected in most translations.

Paul expands on and clarifies the meaning of God's **purpose** in verses 29–30, which will be discussed in the next chapter of this volume. Briefly explained, God's broader **purpose** is to offer salvation to all mankind. As our Lord declared at the beginning of His earthly ministry, "God so loved the world, that He gave His only begotten Son, that whoever believes in Him should not perish, but have eternal life. For God did not send the Son into the world to judge the world, but that the world should be saved through Him" (John 3:16–17). In his second letter, Peter states that the Lord does not desire the condemnation of any person but wants "all to come to repentance" (2 Pet 3:9).

In Romans 8:28, however, Paul is speaking of the narrower, restricted meaning of God's **purpose,** namely, His divine plan to save those whom He has called and "predestined to become conformed to the image of His Son" (v. 29). The focus is on God's sovereign plan of redemption, which He ordained before the foundation of the earth.

While Israel was still wandering in the desert of Sinai, Moses told them, "The Lord did not set His love on you nor choose you because you were more in number than any of the peoples, for you were the fewest of all peoples, but because the Lord loved you and kept the oath which He swore to your forefathers, the Lord brought you out by a mighty hand, and redeemed you from the house of slavery, from the hand of Pharaoh king of Egypt" (Deut 7:7–8). The Jews were not chosen because of who they were but because of who God is. The same is true of God's choosing believers. He chooses solely on the basis of His divine will and **purpose.**

Isaiah wrote, "For I am God, and there is no other; I am God, and there is no one like Me, declaring the end from the beginning and from ancient times things which have not been done, saying, 'My purpose will be established, and I will accomplish all My good pleasure'; calling a bird of prey from the east, the man of My purpose from a far country. Truly I have spoken; truly I will bring it to pass. I have planned it, surely I will do it" (Isa 46:9*b*–11).

John wrote of Jesus, "But as many as received Him, to them He gave the right to become children of God, even to those who believe in His name, who were born not of blood, nor of the will of the flesh, nor of the will of man, but of God" (John 1:12–13).

07

THE ULTIMATE SECURITY—PART 2
THE PURPOSE AND PROGRESS
OF SALVATION

ROMANS 8:29–30

For whom He foreknew, He also predestined to become conformed to the image of His Son, that He might be the firstborn among many brethren; and whom He predestined, these He also called; and whom He called, these He also justified; and whom He justified, these He also glorified. (8:29–30)

From the time of the early church, Christians have debated the possibility of a believer's losing his salvation. Many bitter controversies have centered on that single issue.

As already expressed numerous times in this volume, it is my strong contention that, despite the claims of many sincere believers to the contrary, Scripture is unambiguous in teaching that every person who is genuinely saved is eternally saved. We can never be in danger of losing the spiritual life given to us by God through Jesus Christ. Romans 8:29–30 is perhaps the clearest and most explicit presentation of that truth in all of God's Word. In these two verses Paul reveals the unbroken pattern of God's sovereign redemption, from His eternal foreknowledge of a believer's salvation to its ultimate completion in glorification.

For the sake of easier understanding, the first heading in this chapter will be taken out of textual order. Because the second half of verse 29 states the purpose of the five aspects of salvation that Paul mentions in these two verses, that phrase will be considered first.

THE PURPOSE OF SALVATION

to become conformed to the image of His Son, that He might be the firstborn among many brethren ... (8:29*c*)

Paul introduced the truths of the believer's security and of God's purpose of salvation in the previous verse, stating "God causes all things to work together for good to those who love God, to those who are called according to His purpose" (v. 28). God's calling precedes and makes possible a person's hearing and responding in faith to that divine call. The resulting salvation is made secure by the Lord's causing everything in a believer's life to work for his ultimate good. Conversely, it is impossible for any evil to cause a believer any ultimate harm.

In the middle of verse 29, Paul states the twofold purpose of God's bringing sinners to eternal salvation. The secondary purpose is stated first: to make believers into the likeness of His Son.

TO CONFORM BELIEVERS TO CHRIST

to become conformed to the image of His Son ... (8:29*c*)

From before time began, God chose to save believers from their sins in order that they might **become conformed to the image of His Son,** Jesus Christ. Consequently, every true believer moves inexorably toward perfection in righteousness, as God makes for Himself a people re-created into the likeness of **His** own divine **Son** who will dwell and reign with Him in heaven throughout all eternity. God is redeeming for Himself an eternally holy and Christlike race, to be citizens in His divine kingdom and children in His divine family. For a believer to lose his salvation would be for God to fail in His divine purpose and to condemn to hell those whom He had sovereignly elected to redemption. It would be for God (who cannot lie) to break His covenant with Himself, made before the foundation of the earth. It would mean that the divine seal of the Holy Spirit, imprinted by the King of kings and Lord of lords upon each of His elect children, would be subject to violation and abrogation (see 2 Cor 1:22; Eph 1:13; 4:30).

Leading up to the climactic truth that, without exception, God will complete the salvation of every sinner who is converted to Christ, Paul has already established that "there is therefore now no condemnation for those who are in Christ Jesus" (8:1), that God's Holy Spirit indwells every believer (v. 9), that every believer is already, in this life, an adopted child of God (vv. 14–16), that those children are therefore "heirs of God and fellow heirs with Christ" (v. 17), and that "the Spirit also helps our weakness" and "intercedes for the saints according to the will of God" (Rom 8:26–27).

Building on the categorical declaration that no believer will again face God's condemnation, the apostle progressively establishes that "no condemnation" inevitably eventuates in glorification. There is no failure or partial fulfillment in the sovereign operation of God's salvation plan. Every believer who is saved will one day be glorified. There is absolutely no allowance for the possibility of a believer's sinning himself out of God's grace. He can no more work himself out of salvation than he could have worked himself into it. Nor is there any allowance for an intermediate state of limbo or purgatory, in which some Christians fall short of being fully **conformed to the image of** God's **Son** and must, after death, somehow complete their salvation by their own works or have it completed by others on their behalf.

Although the full truth of it is far too vast and magnificent even for a redeemed human mind to grasp, the New Testament gives us glimpses of what being **conformed to the image** of Christ will be like.

First of all, we will be like Christ *bodily*. One day the Lord will "transform the body of our humble state into conformity with the body of His glory, by the exertion of the power that He has even to subject all things to Himself" (Phil 3:21). As the term itself denotes, glorification (our ultimate conformity to Christ) will be

God's gracious adornment of His children with the very glory of **His** divine **Son.**

The writer of Hebrews tells us that "in these last days [God] has spoken to us in His Son, whom He appointed heir of all things, through whom also He made the world. And He is the radiance of His glory and the exact representation of His nature, and upholds all things by the word of His power. When He had made purification of sins, He sat down at the right hand of the Majesty on high" (Heb 1:2–3). John assures us: "Beloved, now we are children of God, and it has not appeared as yet what we shall be. We know that, when He appears, we shall be like Him, because we shall see Him just as He is" (1 John 3:2). In the meanwhile, as long as we remain on earth, "we all, with unveiled face beholding as in a mirror the glory of the Lord, are being transformed into the same image from glory to glory, just as from the Lord, the Spirit" (2 Cor 3:18). "For if we have become united with Him in the likeness of His death," Paul has explained earlier in Romans, "certainly we shall be also in the likeness of His resurrection" (6:5). "Just as we have borne the image of the earthy, we shall also bear the image of the heavenly" (1 Cor 15:49).

All human beings share a common kind of physical body, but each person has his own distinctive looks and personality. In the same way, the redeemed in heaven will share a common kind of spiritual body but will be individually distinguished from one another. The Bible nowhere teaches the idea that individuality is destroyed at death and that the soul of the deceased becomes absorbed unidentifiably into some cosmic wholeness, or, worse yet, cosmic nothingness. Scripture is clear that, in eternity, both the saved and the damned will retain their individuality. The final resurrection will be of all human beings of all times, a resurrection of life for the righteous and a resurrection of death for the wicked (John 5:29; Acts 24:15).

Second, and more importantly, although not becoming deity, we will be like Christ *spiritually*. Our incorruptible bodies will be infused with the very holiness of Christ, and we will be both outwardly and inwardly perfect, just as our Lord. The writer of Hebrews gives insight into God's gracious plan of redeeming those who believe in His Son and of conforming them to His image when he writes:

> We do see Him who has been made for a little while lower than the angels, namely, Jesus, because of the suffering of death crowned with glory and honor, that by the grace of God He might taste death for everyone. For it was fitting for Him, for whom are all things, and through whom are all things, in bringing many sons to glory, to perfect the author of their salvation through sufferings. For both He who sanctifies and those who are sanctified are all from one Father; for which reason He is not ashamed to call them brethren. (Heb 2:9–11)

TO MAKE CHRIST PREEMINENT

that He might be the firstborn among many brethren ... (8:29*d*)

God's supreme purpose for bringing sinners to salvation is to glorify His Son, Jesus Christ, by making Him preeminent in the divine plan of redemption. In the words of this text, it is God's intent for Christ to **be the firstborn among many brethren.**

In Jewish culture the term **firstborn** always referred to a son, unless a daughter was specifically stated. Because the **firstborn** male child in a Jewish family had a privileged status, the term was often used figuratively to represent preeminence. In the present context that is clearly the meaning.

As it is in almost every instance in the New Testament, the term **brethren** is a synonym for believers. God's primary purpose in His plan of redemption was to make His beloved Son **the firstborn among many brethren** in the sense of Christ's being uniquely preeminent among the children of God. Those who trust in Him become God's adopted children, and Jesus, the true Son of God, graciously deigns to call them His brothers and sisters in God's divine family (Matt 12:50; cf. John 15:15). God's purpose is to make us like Christ in order to create a great redeemed and glorified humanity over which He will reign and be forever preeminent.

In his letter to Philippi, Paul beautifully portrays God's purpose of glorifying Christ: "God highly exalted Him, and bestowed on Him the name which is above every name, that at the name of Jesus every knee should bow, of those who are in heaven, and on earth, and under the earth" (Phil 2:9–10). Our ultimate purpose as the redeemed children of God will be to spend eternity worshiping and giving praise to God's beloved **firstborn,** our preeminent Lord and Savior, Jesus Christ. To the Colossians, Paul further explains that Christ not only is presently the "head of the body, the church," but is also "the beginning, the firstborn from the dead; so that He Himself might come to have first place in everything" (Col 1:18).

God's original purpose in creation was to make a people in His divine image who would give Him honor and glory by serving and obeying Him in all things. But when Adam and Eve rebelled, alienating themselves from God and bringing damnation upon themselves and all subsequent humanity, God had to provide a way of bringing fallen mankind back to Himself.

Through Christ, He provided that way by placing the sins of all mankind upon His sinless Son, causing "the iniquity of us all to fall on Him" (Isa 53:6). Those who trust in that gracious sacrifice on their behalf are saved from their sins and given God's own glory.

As the redeemed of God, conformed to the image of His Son, we will forever glorify Him with the glory He has given us. Like the twenty-four elders who fell down before Christ on His throne, we will cast our crowns of righteousness (2 Tim 4:8), of life (Jas 1:12; Rev 2:10), and of glory (1 Pet 5:4) at our Savior's feet, exclaiming, "Worthy art Thou, our Lord and our God, to receive glory and honor and power; for Thou didst create all things, and because of Thy will they existed, and were created" (Rev 4:10–11).

We thank the Lord for giving us salvation and the eternal life, peace, and joy that salvation brings. But our greatest thanks should be for the unspeakable privilege we have been given of glorifying Christ throughout all eternity.

THE PROGRESS OF SALVATION

For whom He foreknew, He also predestined ... and whom He predestined, these He also called; and whom He called, these He also justified; and whom He justified, these He also glorified. (8:29*a–b*, 30)

In delineating the progress of God's plan of salvation, Paul here briefly states what may be called its five major elements: foreknowledge, predestination, calling, justification, and glorification.

It is essential to realize that these five links in the chain of God's saving work are unbreakable. With the repetition of the connecting phrase **He also,** Paul accentuates that unity by linking each element to the previous one. No one whom God foreknows will fail to be predestined, called, justified, and glorified by Him. It is also significant to note the tense in which the apostle states each element of God's saving work. Paul is speaking here of the Lord's redemptive work from eternity past to eternity future. What he says is true of all believers of all times. Security in Christ is so absolute and unalterable that even the salvation of believers not yet born can be expressed in the past tense, as if it had already occurred. Because God is not bound by time as we are, there is a sense in which the elements not only are sequential but simultaneous. Thus, from His view they are distinct and in another sense are indistinguishable. God has made each of them an indispensable part of the unity of our salvation.

FOREKNOWLEDGE
For whom He foreknew ... (8:29*a*)

Redemption began with God's foreknowledge. A believer is first of all someone **whom He** [God] **foreknew.** Salvation is not initiated by a person's decision to receive Jesus Christ as Lord and Savior. Scripture is clear that repentant faith is essential to salvation and is the first step that *we* take in response to God, but repentant faith does not initiate salvation.

Because Paul is here depicting the plan of salvation from God's perspective, faith is not even mentioned in these two verses.

In His omniscience God is certainly able to look to the end of history and beyond and to know in advance the minutest detail of the most insignificant occurrences. But it is both unbiblical and illogical to argue from that truth that the Lord simply looked ahead to see who would believe and then chose those particular individuals for salvation. If that were true, salvation not only would begin with man's faith but would make God obligated to grant it. In such a scheme, God's initiative would be eliminated and His grace would be vitiated.

That idea also prompts such questions as, "Why then does God create unbelievers if He knows in advance they are going to reject Him?" and "Why doesn't He create only believers?" Another unanswerable question would be, "If God based salvation on His advance knowledge of those who would believe, where did their saving faith come from?" It could not arise from their fallen natures, because the natural, sinful person is at enmity with God (Rom 5:10; 8:7; Eph 2:3; Col 1:21). There is absolutely nothing in man's carnal nature to prompt him to trust in the God against whom he is rebelling. The unsaved person is blind and dead to the things of God. He has absolutely no source of saving faith within himself. "A natural man does not accept the things of the Spirit of God," Paul declares; "for they are foolishness to him, and he cannot understand them, because they are spiritually appraised" (1 Cor 2:14). "The god of this world has blinded the minds of the unbelieving, that they might not see the light of the gospel of the glory of Christ, who is the image of God" (2 Cor 4:4).

The full truth about God's omniscience cannot be comprehended even by believers. No matter how much we may love God and study His Word, we cannot fathom such mysteries. We can only believe what the Bible clearly says—that God does indeed foresee the faith of every person who is saved. We also believe God's revelation that, although men cannot be saved apart from the faithful action of their wills, saving faith, just as every other part of salvation, originates with and is empowered by God alone.

While He was preaching in Galilee early in His ministry, Jesus said, "All that the Father gives Me shall come to Me, and the one who comes to Me I will certainly not cast out" (John 6:37). But lest that statement be interpreted as leaving open the possibility of coming to Him apart from the Father's sending, Jesus later declared categorically that "No one can come to Me, unless the Father who sent Me draws him" (v. 44). New life through the blood of Christ does not come from "the will of the flesh, nor of the will of man, but of God" (John 1:13).

Paul also explains that even faith does not originate with the believer but with God. "For by grace you have been saved through faith; and that not of yourselves, it is the gift of God; not as a result of works, that no one should boast" (Eph 2:8–9).

God's foreknowledge is not a reference to His omniscient foresight but to His foreordination. He not only sees faith in advance but ordains it in advance. Peter had the same reality in mind when he wrote of Christians as those "who are chosen according to the foreknowledge of God the Father" (1 Pet 1:1–2). Peter used the same word "foreknowledge" when he wrote that Christ "was foreknown before the foundation of the world" (1 Pet 1:20). The term means the same thing in both places. Believers were foreknown in the same way Christ was foreknown. That cannot mean foreseen, but must refer to a predetermined choice by God. It is the knowing of predetermined intimate relationship, as when God said to Jeremiah, "Before I formed you in the womb I knew you" (Jer 1:5). Jesus spoke of the same kind of knowing when He said, "I am the good shepherd; and I know My own" (John 10:14).

Because saving faith is foreordained by God, it would have to be that the way of salvation was foreordained, as indeed it was. During his sermon at Pentecost, Peter declared of Christ: "This Man, delivered up by the predetermined plan and foreknowledge of God, you nailed to a cross by the hands of godless men and put Him to death" (Acts 2:23). "Predetermined" is from *horizō*, from which we get the English *horizon*, which designates the outer limits of the earth that we can see from a given vantage point. The basic idea of the Greek term refers to the setting of any boundaries or limits. "Plan" is from *boulē*, a term used in classical Greek to designate an officially convened, decision-making counsel. Both words include the idea of willful intention. "Foreknowledge" is from the noun form of the verb translated **foreknew** in our text. According to what Greek scholars refer to as Granville Sharp's rule, if two nouns of the same case (in this instance, "plan" and "foreknowledge") are connected by *kai* ("and") and have the definite article (the) before the first noun but not before the second, the nouns refer to the same thing (H. E. Dana and Julius R. Mantey, *A Manual Grammar of the Greek New Testament* [New York: Macmillan, 1927], p. 147). In other words, Peter equates God's predetermined plan, or foreordination, and His foreknowledge.

In addition to the idea of foreordination, the term *foreknowledge* also connotes forelove. God has a predetermined divine love for those He plans to save.

Foreknew is from *proginōskō*, a compound word with meaning beyond that of simply knowing beforehand. In Scripture, "to know" often carries the idea of special intimacy and is frequently used of a love relationship. In the statement "Cain had relations with his wife and she conceived" (Gen 4:17), the word behind "had relations with" is the normal Hebrew verb for knowing. It is the same word translated "chosen" in Amos 3:2, where the Lord says to Israel, "You only have I chosen among all the families of the earth." God "knew" Israel in the unique sense of having predetermined that she would be His chosen people. In Matthew's account of Jesus' birth, "kept her a virgin" translates a Greek phrase meaning literally, "did not know her" (Matt 1:25). Jesus used the same word when He warned, "Then I will declare to them, 'I never knew you; depart from Me, you who practice lawlessness'" (Matt 7:23). He was not saying that He had never heard of those unbelievers but that He had no intimate relationship with them as their Savior and Lord. But of believers, Paul says, "The Lord knows those who are His" (2 Tim 2:19).

PREDESTINATION
He also predestined ... (8:29*b*)

From foreknowledge, which looks at the beginning of God's purpose in His act of choosing, God's plan of redemption moves to His predestination, which looks at the end of God's purpose in His act of choosing. *Proorizō* (**predestined**) means literally to mark out, appoint, or determine beforehand. The Lord has predetermined the destiny of every person who will believe in Him. Just as Jesus was crucified "by the predetermined plan and foreknowledge of God" (Acts 2:23), so God **also** has **predestined** every believer to salvation through the means of that atoning sacrifice.

In their prayer of gratitude for the deliverance of Peter and John, a group of believers in Jerusalem praised God for His sovereign power, declaring, "For truly in this city there were gathered together against Thy holy servant Jesus, whom Thou didst anoint, both Herod and Pontius Pilate, along with the Gentiles and the peoples of Israel, to do whatever Thy hand and Thy purpose predestined to occur" (Acts 4:27–28). In other words, the evil and powerful men who nailed Jesus to the cross could not have so much as laid a finger on Him were that not according to God's predetermined plan.

In the opening of his letter to the Ephesian believers, Paul encouraged them with the glorious truth that God "chose us in Him before the foundation of the world, that we should be holy and blameless before Him. In love He predestined us to adoption as sons through Jesus Christ to Himself, according to the kind intention of His will" (Eph 1:4–5).

Much contemporary evangelism gives the impression that salvation is predicated on a person's decision for Christ. But we are not Christians first of all because of what we decided about Christ but because of what God decided about us before the foundation of the world. We were able to choose Him only because He had first chosen us, "according to the kind intention of His will." Paul expresses the same truth a few verses later when he says, "In Him we have redemption through His blood, the forgiveness of our trespasses, according to the riches of His grace, which He lavished upon us. In all wisdom and insight He made known to us the mystery of His will, *according to His kind intention which He purposed in Him*" (Eph 1:7–9, emphasis added). He then says that "we have obtained an inheritance, having been predestined according to His purpose who works all things after the counsel of His will" (v. 11).

CALLING

and whom He predestined, these He also called ...
(8:30*a*)

In God's divine plan of redemption, predestination leads to calling. Although God's calling is also completely by His initiative, it is here that His eternal plan directly intersects our lives in time. Those who are **called** are those in whose hearts the Holy Spirit works to lead them to saving faith in Christ.

As noted under the discussion of verse 28, Paul is speaking in this passage about God's inward call, not the outward call that comes from the proclamation of the gospel. The outward call is essential, because "How shall they believe in Him whom they have not heard?" (Rom 10:14), but that outward call cannot be responded to in faith apart from God's already having inwardly **called** the person through His Spirit.

The Lord's sovereign calling of believers gives still further confirmation that we are eternally secure in Christ. We were saved because God "called us with a holy calling, not according to our works, but according to His own purpose and grace which was granted us in Christ Jesus from all eternity" (2 Tim 1:9). Emphasizing the same truths of the Lord's sovereign purpose in His calling of believers, Paul assured the Thessalonians that "God has chosen you from the beginning for salvation through sanctification by the Spirit and faith in the truth. And it was for this He called you through our gospel, that you may gain the glory of our Lord Jesus Christ" (2 Thess 2:13–14). From beginning to end, our salvation is God's work, not our own. Consequently, we cannot humanly undo what He has divinely done. That is the basis of our security.

It should be strongly emphasized, however, that Scripture nowhere teaches that God chooses unbelievers for condemnation. To our finite minds, that is what would seem to be the corollary of God's calling believers to salvation. But in the divine scheme of things, which far surpasses our understanding, God predestines believers to eternal life, but Scripture *does not* say that He predestines unbelievers to eternal damnation. Although those two truths seem paradoxical to us, we can be sure that they are in perfect divine harmony.

Scripture teaches many truths that seem paradoxical and contradictory. It teaches plainly that God is one, but just as plainly that there are three persons—the Father, the Son, and the Holy Spirit—in the single Godhead. With equal unambiguity the Bible teaches that Jesus Christ is both fully God and fully man. Our finite minds cannot reconcile such seemingly irreconcilable truths, yet they are foundational truths of God's Word.

If a person goes to hell, it is because he rejects God and His way of salvation. "He who believes in Him [Christ] is not judged; he who does not believe has been judged already, because he has not believed in the name of the only begotten Son of God" (John 3:18). As John has declared earlier in his gospel, believers are saved and made children of God "not of blood, nor of the will of the flesh, nor of the will of man, but of God" (John 1:13). But he makes no corresponding statement in regard to unbelievers, nor does any other part of Scripture. Unbelievers are condemned by their own unbelief, not by God's predestination.

Peter makes plain that God does not desire "for any to perish but for all to come to repentance" (2 Pet 3:9). Paul declares with equal clarity: "God our Savior ... desires all men to be saved and to come to the knowledge of the truth" (1 Tim 2:3–4). Every believer is indebted solely to God's grace for his eternal salvation, but every unbeliever is himself solely responsible for his eternal damnation.

God does not choose believers for salvation on the basis of who they are or of what they have done but on the basis of His sovereign grace. For His own reasons alone, God chose Jacob above Esau (Rom 9:13). For His own reasons alone, He chose Israel to be His covenant people (Deut 7:7–8).

We cannot understand God's choosing us for salvation but can only thank and glorify Him for "His grace, which He freely bestowed on us in the Beloved" (Eph 1:6). We can only believe and be forever grateful that we were called "by the grace of Christ" (Gal 1:6) and that "the gifts and the calling of God are irrevocable" (Rom 11:29).

JUSTIFICATION
and whom He called, these He also justified ... (8:30*b*)

The next element of God's saving work is justification of those who believe. After they are **called** by God, they are **also justified** by Him. And just as foreknowledge, predestination, and calling are the exclusive work of God, so is justification.

Because justification is discussed in considerable detail in chapters 17–18 of this volume, it is necessary here simply to point out that **justified** refers to a believer's being made right *with* God *by* God. Because "all have sinned and fall short of the glory of God," men can only be "justified as a gift by [God's] grace through the redemption which is in Christ Jesus" (Rom 3:24).

GLORIFICATION

and whom He justified, these He also glorified. (8:30*c*)

As with foreknowledge, predestination, calling, and justification, glorification is inseparable from the other elements and is exclusively a work of God.

In saying that those **whom He justified, these He also glorified,** Paul again emphasizes the believer's eternal security. As noted above, no one whom God foreknows will fail to be predestined, called, justified, and ultimately **glorified.** As believers, we know with absolute certainty that awaiting us is "an eternal weight of glory far beyond all comparison" (2 Cor 4:17).

Ultimate glory has been a recurring theme throughout Paul's epistle to the Romans. In 5:2 he wrote, "We exult in hope of the glory of God." In 8:18 he said, "I consider that the sufferings of this present time are not worthy to be compared with the glory that is to be revealed to us." He anticipated that marvelous day when "creation itself also will be set free from its slavery to corruption into the freedom of the glory of the children of God" (8:21).

To the Thessalonians Paul wrote that our ultimate glorification is the very purpose for which we are redeemed: "It was for this He called you through our gospel, that you may gain the glory of our Lord Jesus Christ" (2 Thess 2:14).

This promise of final glory was no uncertain hope as far as Paul was concerned. By putting the phrase **these He also glorified** in the past tense, the apostle demonstrated his own conviction that everyone **whom He justified** is eternally secure. Those who "obtain the salvation which is in Christ Jesus [receive] with it eternal glory" (2 Tim 2:10). That is God's own guarantee.

08

THE HYMN OF SECURITY

ROMANS 8:31–39

W hat then shall we say to these things? If God is for us, who is against us? He who did not spare His own Son, but delivered Him up for us all, how will He not also with Him freely give us all things? Who will bring a charge against God's elect? God is the one who justifies; who is the one who condemns? Christ Jesus is He who died, yes, rather who was raised, who is at the right hand of God, who also intercedes for us. Who shall separate us from the love of Christ? Shall tribulation, or distress, or persecution, or famine, or nakedness, or peril, or sword? Just as it is written, "For Thy sake we are being put to death all day long; we were considered as sheep to be slaughtered." But in all these things we overwhelmingly conquer through Him who loved us. For I am convinced that neither death, nor life, nor angels, nor principalities, nor things present, nor things to come, nor powers, nor height, nor depth, nor any other created thing, shall be able to separate us from the love of God, which is in Christ Jesus our Lord. (8:31–39)

Paul closes this magnificent chapter with what might be called a hymn of security. With all the apostle has said previously in this chapter 36 about security, especially after his climactic declarations in verses 28–30, it would seem there was nothing left to add. But this closing passage is a crescendo of questions and answers regarding issues some objectors might still raise. Although verses 31–39 continue his argument in defense of security, they also amount to an almost poetic declaration of thanksgiving for God's grace, in which His children will live and rejoice throughout all eternity.

THE INTRODUCTION

What then shall we say to these things? (8:31*a*)

Judging from what Paul says in the rest of the passage, **these things** doubtless refer to the issues he has already dealt with in the chapter. Much of what he says in verses 31–39 relates to the doctrine of Christ's substitutionary atonement, but the specific focus is still on the security that His atonement brings to those who believe in Him.

Paul realizes that many fearful believers will still have doubts about their security and that false teachers would be ready to exploit those doubts. To give such believers the assurance they need, the apostle reveals God's answer to two closely related questions: Can any person or can any circumstance cause a believer to lose his salvation?

PERSONS WHO MIGHT SEEM TO
THREATEN OUR SECURITY

If God is for us, who is against us? He who did not spare His own Son, but delivered Him up for us all, how will He not also with Him freely give us all things? Who will bring a charge against God's elect? God is the one who justifies; who is the one who condemns? Christ Jesus is He who died, yes, rather who was raised, who is at the right hand of God, who also intercedes for us. (8:31*b*–34)

Paul begins with an all-encompassing rhetorical question, **If God is for us, who is against us?** The word **if** translates the Greek conditional particle *ei*, signifying a fulfilled condition, not a mere possibility. The meaning of the first clause is therefore "*Because* **God is for us.**"

The obvious implication is that if anyone were able to rob us of salvation they would have to be greater than God Himself, because He is both the giver and the sustainer of salvation. To Christians Paul is asking, in effect, "Who could conceivably take away our no-condemnation status?" (see 8:1). Is there anyone stronger than God, the Creator of everything and everyone who exists?

David declared with unreserved confidence, "The Lord is my light and my salvation; whom shall I fear? The Lord is the defense of my life; whom shall I dread?"

(Ps 27:1). In another psalm we read, "God is our refuge and strength, a very present help in trouble. Therefore we will not fear, though the earth should change, and though the mountains slip into the heart of the sea; though its waters roar and foam, though the mountains quake at its swelling pride.... The Lord of hosts is with us; the God of Jacob is our stronghold" (Ps 46:1–3, 11).

Proclaiming the immeasurable greatness of God, Isaiah wrote,

> It is He who sits above the vault of the earth, and its inhabitants are like grasshoppers, who stretches out the heavens like a curtain and spreads them out like a tent to dwell in.... Lift up your eyes on high and see who has created these stars, the One who leads forth their host by number, He calls them all by name; because of the greatness of His might and the strength of His power not one of them is missing.... Do you not know? Have you not heard? The Everlasting God, the Lord, the Creator of the ends of the earth does not become weary or tired. His understanding is inscrutable. (Isa 40:22, 26, 28)

In Romans 8:31 Paul does not specify any particular persons who might be successful against us, but it would be helpful to consider some of the possibilities.

First of all, we might wonder, "Can other people rob us of salvation?" Many of Paul's initial readers of this epistle were Jewish and would be familiar with the Judaizing heresy promulgated by highly legalistic Jews who claimed to be Christians. They insisted that no person, Jew or Gentile, could be saved or maintain his salvation without strict observance of the Mosaic law, and especially circumcision.

The Jerusalem Council was called to discuss that very issue, and its binding decision was that no Christian is under the ritual law of the Mosaic covenant (see Acts 15:1–29). The major thrust of Paul's letter to the churches in Galatia was against the Judaizing heresy and is summarized in the following passage:

> If you receive circumcision, Christ will be of no benefit to you. And I testify again to every man who receives circumcision, that he is under obligation to keep the whole Law. You have been severed from Christ, you who are seeking to be justified by law; you have fallen from grace. For we through the Spirit, by faith, are waiting for the hope of righteousness. For in Christ Jesus neither circumcision nor uncircumcision means anything, but faith working through love. (Gal 5:2–6; cf. 2:11–16; 3:1–15)

The Roman Catholic church teaches that salvation can be lost by committing so-called mortal sins and also claims power for itself both to grant and to revoke grace. But such ideas have no foundation in Scripture and are thoroughly heretical. No person or group of persons, regardless of their ecclesiastical status, can bestow or withdraw the smallest part of God's grace.

When Paul was bidding farewell to the Ephesian elders who had come to meet him at Miletus, he warned, "Be on guard for yourselves and for all the flock, among which the Holy Spirit has made you overseers, to shepherd the church of God which He purchased with His own blood. I know that after my departure savage wolves will come in among you, not sparing the flock; and from among your own selves men will arise, speaking perverse things, to draw away the disciples after them" (Acts 20:28–30). Paul was not suggesting that true believers can be robbed of salvation but was warning that they can be seriously misled, confused, and weakened in their faith and that the cause of the gospel can be greatly hindered. Although false teaching cannot prevent the completion of a believer's salvation, it can easily confuse an unbeliever regarding salvation.

Second, we might wonder if Christians can put themselves out of God's grace by committing some unusually heinous sin that nullifies the divine work of redemption that binds them to the Lord. Tragically, some evangelical churches teach that loss of salvation is possible. But if we were not able by our own power or effort to save ourselves—to free ourselves from sin, to bring ourselves to God, and to make ourselves His children—how could it be that by our own efforts we could nullify the work of grace that God Himself has accomplished in us?

Third, we might wonder if God the Father would take away our salvation. It was, after all, the Father who "so loved the world, that He gave His only begotten Son, that whoever believes in Him should not perish, but have eternal life" (John 3:16). If anyone could take away salvation, it would have to be the One who gave it. We might argue theoretically that, because God is sovereign and omnipotent, He *could* take away salvation if He wanted to. But the idea that He *would* do that flies in the face of Scripture, including the present text.

In answer to such a suggestion, Paul asks, **He who did not spare His own Son, but delivered Him up for us all, how will He not also with Him freely give us all things?** How could it possibly be that God would sacrifice His own Son for the sake of those who believe in Him and then cast some of those blood-bought believers out of His family and His kingdom? Would God do less for believers after they are saved than He did for them prior to salvation? Would He do less for His children than He did for His enemies? If God loved us so much while we were wretched sinners that He delivered up **His own Son ... for us,** would He turn His back on us after we have been cleansed from sin and made righteous in His sight?

Isaac was an Old Testament picture of Christ. When God commanded Abraham to sacrifice Isaac, the only son of promise, both Abraham and Isaac willingly obeyed. Abraham's willingness to sacrifice Isaac is a beautiful foreshadow of God the Father's willingness to offer up His only begotten Son as a sacrifice for the sins of the world. Isaac's willingness to be sacrificed foreshadows Christ's willingness to go to the cross.

God intervened to spare Isaac and provided a ram in his place (Gen 22:1–13). At that point, however, the analogy changes from comparison to contrast, because God **did not spare His own Son, but delivered Him up for us all.**

Isaiah extoled the wondrous love of both God the Father and God the Son when he wrote,

> Surely our griefs He Himself [Christ, the Son] bore, and our sorrows He carried; yet we ourselves esteemed Him stricken, smitten of God [the Father], and afflicted. But He was pierced through for our transgressions, He was crushed for our iniquities; the chastening for our well-being fell upon Him, and by His scourging we are healed. All of us like sheep have gone astray, each of us has turned to his own way; but the Lord has caused the iniquity of us all to fall on Him.... But the Lord [the Father] was pleased to crush Him [the Son], putting Him to grief; if He would render Himself as a guilt offering. (Isa 53:4–6, 10)

Jesus' sacrifice on the cross not only is the foundation of our salvation but also of our security. Because the Father loved us so much while we were still under condemnation, "He made Him who knew no sin to be sin on our behalf, that we might become the righteousness of God in Him" (2 Cor 5:21). Because the Son loved us so much while we were still under condemnation, He "gave Himself for our sins, that He might deliver us out of this present evil age, according to the will of our God and Father" (Gal 1:4; cf. 3:13).

Jesus promises all those who belong to Him: "In My Father's house are many dwelling places; if it were not so, I would have told you; for I go to prepare a place for you. And if I go and prepare a place for you, I will come again, and receive you to Myself; that where I am, there you may be also" (John 14:2–3). The Lord makes no allowance for *any* of His people to be lost again, but promises each one of them an eternal home in His eternal presence. Jesus also assures us that the Holy Spirit will be with us forever (John 14:16), again making no allowance for exceptions. What power in heaven or earth could rob the Godhead of those who have been divinely saved for eternity?

Beginning in verse 8 of chapter 12, Paul speaks almost entirely in the first and second persons, referring to himself and to fellow believers. It is the same spiritual brethren (**us**) he speaks of twice in verse 32. If the Father delivered up His Son **for us all,** he argues, **how will He not also with Him freely give us all things?** In his letter to Ephesus the apostle is also speaking of fellow believers when he says, "Blessed be the God and Father of our Lord Jesus Christ, who has blessed us with every spiritual blessing in the heavenly places in Christ" (Eph 1:3). If God blesses **all of us,** His children, with "every spiritual blessing in the heavenly places in Christ," loss of salvation is clearly impossible. All believers receive that eternal inheritance.

Freely give translates *charizomai*, which means to bestow graciously or out of grace. In some of Paul's other letters the same word carries the idea of forgiveness (see 2 Cor 2:7, 10; 12:13; Col 2:13; 3:13). It therefore seems reasonable to interpret Paul's use of *charizomai* in Romans 8:32 as including the idea of God's gracious forgiveness as well as His gracious giving. If so, the apostle is also saying that God **freely** *forgives* **us all things** (cf. 1 John 1:9). God's unlimited forgiveness makes it impossible for a believer to sin himself out of God's grace.

In order to assure His people of their security in Him, "in the same way God, desiring even more to show to the heirs of the promise the unchangeableness of His purpose, interposed with an oath, in order that by two unchangeable things, in which it is impossible for God to lie, we may have strong encouragement, we who have fled for refuge in laying hold of the hope set before us" (Heb 6:17–18). The two unchangeable features of God's unchangeable purpose are His promise and His oath to honor that promise. What greater proof of security could we have than the unchangeable purpose of God to save and keep His elect, the heirs of promise?

Fourth, we might wonder if Satan can take away our salvation. Because he is our most powerful supernatural enemy, if anyone other than God could rob us of salvation, it would surely be the devil. He is

called "the accuser of [the] brethren" (Rev 12:10), and
the book of Job depicts him clearly in that role:

> And the Lord said to Satan, "Have you considered My servant
> Job? For there is no one like him on the earth, a blameless and
> upright man, fearing God and turning away from evil." Then
> Satan answered the Lord, "Does Job fear God for nothing? Hast
> Thou not made a hedge about him and his house and all that
> he has, on every side? Thou hast blessed the work of his hands,
> and his possessions have increased in the land. But put forth
> Thy hand now and touch all that he has; he will surely curse
> Thee to Thy face. (Job 1:8–11)

Satan accused Job of worshiping God out of
selfishness rather than out of reverence and love.
Although Job at one point questioned God's wisdom
and was divinely rebuked (chaps. 38–41), he repented
and was forgiven. From the beginning to the end of Job's
testing, the Lord affectionately called him "My servant"
(see 1:8; 42:7–8). Although Job's faith was not perfect,
it was genuine. The Lord therefore permitted Satan to
test Job, but He knew Satan could never destroy Job's
persevering faith or rob His servant of salvation.

In one of his visions, the prophet Zechariah reports:
"Then he [an angel] showed me Joshua the high priest
standing before the angel of the Lord, and Satan
standing at his right hand to accuse him. And the Lord
said to Satan, 'The Lord rebuke you, Satan! Indeed,the
Lord who has chosen Jerusalem rebuke you! Is this not

a brand plucked from the fire?'" (Zech 3:1–2). Although "Joshua was clothed with filthy garments" (v. 3), that is, was still living with the sinful flesh, he was one of the Lord's redeemed and was beyond Satan's power to destroy or discredit.

Satan also tried to undermine Peter's faith, and Jesus warned him of that danger, saying, "Simon, Simon, behold, Satan has demanded permission to sift you like wheat." He then assured the apostle, "but I have prayed for you, that your faith may not fail" (Luke 22:31–32).

Because every believer has that divine protection, Paul asks, **Who will bring a charge against God's elect? God is the one who justifies; who is the one who condemns?** The world and Satan are continually bringing charges **against God's elect,** but those charges amount to nothing before the Lord, because He **is the one who justifies,** the one who decides who is righteous before Him. They have been declared eternally guiltless and are no longer under the condemnation of God (8:1), the only **one who condemns.** God conceived the law, revealed the law, interprets the law, and applies the law. And through the sacrifice of His Son, all the demands of the law have been met for those who trust in Him.

That great truth inspired Count Zinzendorf to write the following lines in the glorious hymn "Jesus, Thy Blood and Righteousness," translated by John Wesley:

> Bold shall I stand in that great day,
> For who ought to my charge shall lay?
> Fully absolved through Thee I am
> From sin and fear, from guilt and shame.

It is not that the accusations made against believers by Satan and the unbelieving world are always false. The fact that we are not yet sinless is obvious. But even when a charge against us is true, it is never sufficient grounds for our damnation, because all our sins—past, present, and future—have been covered by the blood of Christ and we are now clothed in His righteousness.

Fifth, we might wonder if our Savior Himself would take back our salvation. Anticipating that question, Paul declares, **Christ Jesus is He who died, yes, rather who was raised, who is at the right hand of God, who also intercedes for us.** It is because Jesus makes continuous intercession for *all* believers, **God's elect,** that "they shall never perish" and that "no one shall snatch them out of [His] hand" (John 10:28). For **Christ** to take away our salvation would be for Him to work against Himself and to nullify His own promise. Christ offers no temporary spiritual life but only that which is eternal. He could not grant eternal life and then take it away, because that would demonstrate that the life He had granted was *not* eternal.

In verse 34 Paul reveals four realities that protect our salvation in Jesus Christ. First, he says that **Christ**

Jesus ... died. In His death He took upon Himself the full penalty for our sins. In His death He bore the condemnation that we deserved but from which we are forever freed (8:1). The death of the Lord Jesus Christ on our behalf is the only condemnation we will ever know.

Second, Christ **was raised** from the dead, proving His victory over sin and over its supreme penalty of death. The grave could not hold Jesus, because He had conquered death; and His conquest over death bequeaths eternal life to every person who trusts in Him. As Paul has declared earlier in this letter, Christ "was delivered up because of our transgressions, and was raised because of our justification" (Rom 4:25). His death paid the price for our sins and His resurrection gave absolute proof that the price was paid. When God raised Jesus from the dead, He demonstrated that His Son had offered the full satisfaction for sin that the law demands.

Third, Christ **is at the right hand of God,** the place of divine exaltation and honor. Because "He humbled Himself by becoming obedient to the point of death, even death on a cross, ... God highly exalted Him, and bestowed on Him the name which is above every name" (Phil 2:8–9). David foretold that glorious event when he wrote, "The Lord says to my Lord: 'Sit at My right hand, until I make Thine enemies a footstool for Thy feet'" (Ps 110:1).

There were no seats in the Temple, because the sacrifices made there by the priests were never finished. They were but pictures of the one and only true sacrifice that the Son of God one day would make. The writer of Hebrews explains that "every priest stands daily ministering and offering time after time the same sacrifices, which can never take away sins; but He [Christ], having offered one sacrifice for sins for all time, sat down at the right hand of God" (Heb 10:11–12; cf. 1:3).

Fourth, Christ **also intercedes for us.** Although His work of atonement was finished, His continuing ministry of intercession for those saved through His sacrifice will continue without interruption until every redeemed soul is safe in heaven. Just as Isaiah had prophesied, "He poured out Himself to death, and was numbered with the transgressors; yet He Himself bore the sin of many, and interceded for the transgressors" (Isa 53:12). Jesus Christ "is able to save forever those who draw near to God through Him, since He always lives to make intercession for them" (Heb 7:25).

If we understand what Christ did on the cross to save us from sin, we understand what it means to be secure in His salvation. If we believe that God loved us so much when we were wretched and ungodly that He sent His Son to die on the cross to bring us to Himself, how could we believe that, after we are saved, His love is not strong enough to keep us saved? If Christ had power to redeem us out of bondage to sin, how could He lack power to keep us redeemed?

Christ, the perfect Priest, offered a perfect sacrifice to make us perfect. To deny the security of the believer is therefore to deny the sufficiency of the work of Christ. To deny the security of the believer is to misunderstand the heart of God, to misunderstand the gift of Christ, to misunderstand the meaning of the cross, to misunderstand the biblical meaning of salvation.

Even when we sin after we are saved, "if we confess our sins, He is faithful and righteous to forgive us our sins and to cleanse us from all unrighteousness," because in Him "we have an Advocate with the Father, Jesus Christ the righteous" (1 John 1:9; 2:1). When we sin, our Lord intercedes on our behalf and comes to our defense against Satan and any others who might bring charges against us (see Rom 8:33). "God is able to make all grace abound to you," Paul assured the believers at Corinth (2 Cor 9:8). Through our remaining days on earth and throughout all eternity, our gracious Lord will hold us safe in His everlasting love by His everlasting power.

CIRCUMSTANCES THAT MIGHT SEEM TO THREATEN OUR SECURITY

Who shall separate us from the love of Christ? Shall tribulation, or distress, or persecution, or famine, or nakedness, or peril, or sword? Just as it is written, "For Thy sake we are being put to death all day long; we were considered as sheep

to be slaughtered." But in all these things we overwhelmingly conquer through Him who loved us. (8:35–37)

After establishing that it is impossible for any person to take away our salvation, Paul anticipates a similar question that some will ask: "Is it possible for circumstances to rob a believer of his salvation?" The apostle now proceeds to show that that, too, is impossible.

The interrogative pronoun *tis* (**who**) is the same word that begins the previous two verses. But the Greek term also can mean "what," and the fact that Paul speaks only of things and not people in verses 35–37, makes clear that he is now referring to impersonal things.

Unpleasant and dangerous circumstances obviously can have a detrimental influence on the faith and endurance of believers. The question here, however, is whether they can cause a believer to sin himself out of salvation. In essence, this question is an extension of the one discussed above regarding the possibility of a believer's dislodging himself from God's grace.

Paul anticipates and refutes the notion that any circumstance, no matter how threatening and potentially destructive, can cause a genuine believer to forfeit his salvation. In verse 35 Paul lists a representative few of the countless ominous circumstances that faithful believers may encounter while they still live in the world.

First of all, it should be noted that **the love of Christ** does not refer to the believer's love for Him but rather to His love for the believer (see vv. 37, 39). No person can love Christ who has not experienced the redeeming work of Christ's love for him: "We love, because He first loved us" (1 John 4:19).

In this context, **the love of Christ** represents salvation. Paul is therefore asking rhetorically if any circumstance is powerful enough to cause a true believer to turn against **Christ** in a way that would cause **Christ** to turn His back on the believer. At issue, then, are the power and permanence of **the love of Christ** for those He has bought with His own blood and brought into the family and the kingdom of His Father.

John reports that "Before the Feast of the Passover, Jesus knowing that His hour had come that He should depart out of this world to the Father, having loved His own who were in the world, He loved them to the end" (John 13:1). As John makes clear in his first epistle, "the end" does not refer simply to the end of Jesus' earthly life but to the end of every believer's earthly life. "By this the love of God was manifested in us, that God has sent His only begotten Son into the world so that we might live through Him. In this is love, not that we loved God, but that He loved us and sent His Son to be the propitiation for our sins.... By this, love is perfected with us, that we may have confidence in the day of judgment; because as He is, so also are we in this world" (1 John 4:9–10, 17). We have confidence as we face the day of judgment, because we know that the divine and indestructible love of Christ binds us eternally to Him.

In a majestic benediction at the end of the second chapter of his second letter to Thessalonica, Paul says, "Now may our Lord Jesus Christ Himself and God our Father, who has loved us and given us eternal comfort and good hope by grace, comfort and strengthen your hearts in every good work and word" (2 Thess 2:16–17). Eternal comfort and good hope are the permanent gifts of God's grace, because, by definition, that which is eternal cannot end.

The first threatening circumstance Paul mentions is **tribulation,** from *thlipsis*, which carries the idea of being squeezed or placed under pressure. In Scripture the word is perhaps most often used of outward difficulties, but it is also used of emotional stress. The idea here is probably that of severe adversity in general, the kind that is common to all men.

The second threatening circumstance is **distress,** which translates the compound Greek word *stenochōria*, which is composed of the terms for narrow and space. The idea is similar to that of tribulation and carries the primary idea of strict confinement, of being helplessly hemmed in. In such circumstances a believer can only trust in the Lord and pray for the power to endure. Sometimes we are caught in situations where we are continually confronted with temptations we cannot avoid. Paul counsels believers who are under such **distress** to remember that "no temptation has overtaken you but such as is common to man; and God is faithful, who will not allow you to be tempted beyond what you are able, but with the temptation will provide the way of escape also, that you may be able to endure it" (1 Cor 10:13). Until He provides a way of escape, the Lord provides the power to resist.

The third threatening circumstance is **persecution,** which refers to affliction suffered for the sake of Christ. Persecution is never pleasant, but in the Beatitudes Jesus gives a double promise of God's blessing us when we suffer for His sake. He then bids us to "rejoice, and be glad, for your reward in heaven is great, for so they persecuted the prophets who were before you" (Matt 5:10–12).

Famine often results from persecution, when Christians are discriminated against in employment and cannot afford to buy enough food to eat. Many believers have been imprisoned for their faith and have gradually starved to death because of inadequate food.

Nakedness does not refer to complete nudity but to destitution in which a person cannot adequately clothe himself. It also suggests the idea of being vulnerable and unprotected.

To be in **peril** is simply to be exposed to danger in general, including danger from treachery and mistreatment.

The **sword** to which Paul refers was more like a large dagger and was frequently used by assassins, because it was easily concealed. It was a symbol of death and suggests being murdered rather than dying in military battle.

Paul was not speaking of these afflictions in theory or secondhand. He himself had faced those hardships and many more, as he reports so vividly in 2 Corinthians 11. Referring to certain Jewish leaders in the church who were boasting of their suffering for Christ, Paul writes,

> Are they servants of Christ? (I speak as if insane) I more so; in far more labors, in far more imprisonments, beaten times without number, often in danger of death. Five times I received from the Jews thirty-nine lashes. Three times I was beaten with rods, once I was stoned, three times I was shipwrecked, a night and a day I have spent in the deep. I have been on frequent journeys, in dangers from rivers, dangers from robbers, dangers from my countrymen, dangers from the Gentiles, dangers in the city, dangers in the wilderness, dangers on the sea, dangers among false brethren; I have been in labor and hardship, through many sleepless nights, in hunger and thirst, often without food, in cold and exposure. (vv. 23–27)

Quoting from the Septuagint (Greek Old Testament) version of Psalm 44:22, Paul continues,

just as it is written, "For Thy sake we are being put to death all day long; we were considered as sheep to be slaughtered." In other words, Christians should not be surprised when they have to endure suffering for the sake of Christ.

Before Paul wrote this epistle, God's faithful people had suffered for centuries, not only at the hands of Gentiles but also at the hands of fellow Jews. They "experienced mockings and scourgings, yes, also chains and imprisonment. They were stoned, they were sawn in two, they were tempted, they were put to death with the sword; they went about in sheepskins, in goatskins, being destitute, afflicted, ill-treated (men of whom the world was not worthy), wandering in deserts and mountains and caves and holes in the ground" (Heb 11:36–38).

The cost of faithfulness to God has always been high. Jesus declared, "He who loves father or mother more than Me is not worthy of Me; and he who loves son or daughter more than Me is not worthy of Me. And he who does not take his cross and follow after Me is not worthy of Me. He who has found his life shall lose it, and he who has lost his life for My sake shall find it" (Matt 10:37–39). Paul assured his beloved Timothy that "indeed, all who desire to live godly in Christ Jesus will be persecuted" (2 Tim 3:12).

If a professing Christian turns his back on the things of God or lives persistently in sin, he proves that he never belonged to Christ at all. Such people have not lost their salvation but have never received it. About such nominal Christians, John said, "They went out from us, but they were not really of us; for if they had been of us, they would have remained with us; but they went out, in order that it might be shown that they all are not of us" (1 John 2:19).

If the things of the world continually keep a person from the things of God, that person proves he is not a child of God. During Jesus' earthly ministry, many thousands of people walked great distances to hear Him preach and to receive physical healing for themselves and their loved ones. At His triumphal entry into Jerusalem, the crowd acclaimed Him as their Messiah and wanted to make Him king. But after He was convicted and crucified, and the cost of true discipleship became evident, most of those who had once hailed Christ were nowhere to be found.

Luke gives an account of three men, doubtless representative of many others, who professed allegiance to Jesus but who would not submit to His lordship and thereby proved their lack of saving faith. The first man, whom Matthew identifies as a scribe (8:19), promised to follow Jesus wherever He went. But knowing the man's heart, "Jesus said to him, 'The foxes have holes, and the birds of the air have nests, but the Son of Man has nowhere to lay His head'" (9:57–58). When the Lord called a second man, he asked permission to first bury his father. He did not mean that his father had just died but rather that he wanted to postpone commitment to Christ until after his father eventually died, at which time the son would receive his family inheritance. Jesus "said to him, 'Allow the dead to bury their own dead; but as for you, go and proclaim everywhere the kingdom of God' " (vv. 59–60). In other words, let those who are spiritually dead take care of their own carnal interests. The third man wanted to follow Jesus after he said "goodbye to those at home." To Him the Lord replied, "No one, after putting his hand to the plow and looking back, is fit for the kingdom of God" (vv. 61–62).

We are not told what any of the three men eventually did in regard to following Christ, but the implication is that, like the rich young man (Matt 19:22), the cost of true discipleship, which is always the mark of true salvation, was too high for them.

Only the true believer perseveres, not because he is strong in himself but because he has the power of God's indwelling Spirit. His perseverance does not keep his salvation safe but proves that his salvation *is* safe. Those who fail to persevere not only demonstrate their lack of courage but, much more importantly, their lack of genuine faith. God will keep and protect even the most fearful person who truly belongs to Him. On the other hand, even the bravest of those who are merely professing Christians will invariably fall away when the cost of being identified with Christ becomes too great.

Only true Christians are overcomers because only true Christians have the divine help of Christ's own Spirit. "For we have become partakers of Christ," explains the writer of Hebrews, "if we hold fast the beginning of our assurance firm until the end" (Heb 3:14). To some Jews who believed Him, Jesus said, "If you abide in My word, then you are truly disciples of Mine; and you shall know the truth, and the truth shall make you free" (John 8:31–32). Holding fast and abiding in God's Word neither merit nor preserve salvation. But the presence of those virtues confirms the reality of salvation, and the absence of them confirms the condition of lostness.

Just as we can only love God because He first loved us, we can only hold on to God because He holds on to us. We can survive any threatening circumstance and overcome any spiritual obstacle that the world or Satan puts in our way because **in all these things we overwhelmingly conquer through Him who loved us.**

Overwhelmingly conquer is from *hupernikaō*, a compound verb that literally means to hyper-conquer, to over-conquer, to conquer, as it were, with success to spare. Those who **overwhelmingly conquer** are supremely victorious in overcoming everyone and everything that threatens their relationship to Jesus Christ. But they do so entirely **through** His power, the power of **Him who loved us** so much that He gave His life for us that we might have life in Him.

Because our Lord both saves and keeps us, we do much more than simply endure and survive the ominous circumstances Paul mentions in verse 35. First of all, we **overwhelmingly conquer** by coming out of troubles stronger than when they first threatened us. Paul has just declared that, by His divine grace and power, God causes everything, including the very worst things, to work for the good of His children (8:28). Even when we suffer because of our own sinfulness or unfaithfulness, our gracious Lord will bring us through with a deeper understanding of our own unrighteousness and of His perfect righteousness, of our own faithlessness and of His steadfast faithfulness, of our own weakness and of His great power.

Second, we **overwhelmingly conquer** because our ultimate reward will far surpass whatever earthly and temporal loss we may suffer. With Paul, we should view even the most terrible circumstance as but "momentary, light affliction" that produces "for us an eternal weight of glory far beyond all comparison" (2 Cor 4:17).

From the human perspective, of course, the over-conquest God promises often seems a long time in coming. But when, as true believers, we go through times of testing, whatever their nature or cause, we come out spiritually refined by our Lord. Instead of those things separating us from Christ, they will bring us closer to Him. His grace and glory will rest on us and we will grow in our understanding of His will and of the sufficiency of His grace. While we wait for Him to bring us through the trials, we know that He says to us what He said to Paul, "My grace is sufficient for you, for power is perfected in weakness." And we should respond with Paul, "Most gladly, therefore, I will rather boast about my weaknesses, that the power of Christ may dwell in me" (2 Cor 12:9).

Paul probably wrote his letter to Rome during a winter in Corinth, and it is not likely that either Paul or the Roman believers realized how short the time would be before they would stand in need of the apostle's comforting words in this passage. It would not be many years before they would face fierce persecution from a pagan government and people that now tolerated them with indifference. It would not be long before the blood of those to whom this epistle is addressed would soak the sands of Roman amphitheaters. Some would be mauled by wild beasts, some would be slain by ruthless gladiators, and others would be used as human torches to light Nero's garden parties.

Consequently, the true and false believers soon would be easily distinguished. Many congregations would be saying of former members, "They went out from us, but they were not really of us; for if they had been of us, they would have remained with us; but they went out, in order that it might be shown that they all are not of us" (1 John 2:19). But those whom the world looks upon as the overwhelmed and conquered are in reality overwhelming conquerors. In God's scheme of things, the victors are the vanquished and the vanquished are the victors.

THE CONCLUSION

For I am convinced that neither death, nor life, nor angels, nor principalities, nor things present, nor things to come, nor powers, nor height, nor depth, nor any other created thing, shall be able to separate us from the love of God, which is in Christ Jesus our Lord. (8:38–39)

This chapter closes with a beautiful summary of what has just been said. The apostle assures his readers that he was not teaching them anything about which he himself was not fully **convinced.** He was convinced first of all because of the nature of salvation, which God had revealed to him and which he presents so clearly in these first eight chapters. His counsel is also a personal testimony. He was convinced because he had experienced most of the things mentioned and they did not separate him from Christ. Both revelation and experience convinced him. Paul was saying to believers in Rome the same thing he would say some years later to Timothy: "For this reason I also suffer these things, but I am not ashamed; for I know whom I have believed and I am convinced that He is able to guard what I have entrusted to Him until that day" (2 Tim 1:12).

Paul begins his list with **death,** which, in our earthly life, we experience last. Even that supreme enemy cannot separate us from our Lord, because He has changed death's sting from defeat to victory. We can therefore rejoice in the psalmist's affirmation that "precious in the sight of the Lord is the death of His godly ones" (Ps 116:15), and we can testify with David that "even though I walk through the valley of the shadow of death, I fear no evil; for Thou art with me; Thy rod and Thy staff, they comfort me" (Ps 23:4). With Paul, we should "prefer rather to be absent from the body" because that will mean we are finally "at home with the Lord" (2 Cor 5:8).

Donald Grey Barnhouse told a personal story that beautifully illustrates death's powerlessness over Christians. When his wife died, his children were still quite young, and Dr. Barnhouse wondered how he could explain their mother's death in a way their childish minds could understand. As they drove home from the funeral, a large truck passed them and briefly cast a dark shadow over the car. Immediately the father had the illustration he was looking for, and he asked the children, "Would you rather be run over by a truck or by the shadow of a truck?" "That's easy, Daddy," they replied. "We would rather get run over by the shadow, because that wouldn't hurt." Their father then said, "Well, children, your mother just went through the valley of the shadow of death, and there's no pain there, either."

The second supposed hindrance does not seem like a hindrance at all. We think of **life** as something positive. But it is in our present earthly **life** that spiritual dangers lie. Not only does death itself hold no harm for believers, but it will bring the end of all harm. It is while we still have *this* **life** that we face tribulation, distress, persecution, famine, nakedness, peril, sword (8:35) and the many other trials that Paul could have mentioned. But because we have eternal life in Christ, the threats during our present **life** are empty.

The third supposed threat is **angels.** Because the next danger on the list (**principalities**) doubtless refers to fallen angels, it seems likely that the ones mentioned here are holy **angels.** Paul's reference here to angels presupposes a purely hypothetical and impossible situation, just as did one of his warnings to the Galatians. He told the Galatian believers to stand firm in their salvation through Christ's shed blood on the cross and to refuse to accept any contrary gospel, even if preached, if that were possible, by an apostle or "an angel from heaven" (Gal 1:8).

The fourth supposed threat is not in the least hypothetical. As already noted, **principalities** seems to refer to evil beings, specifically demons. Like the Greek term (*archē*) behind it, **principalities** indicates neither good nor evil. But the obvious negative use of *archē* in such passages as Ephesians 6:12 ("rulers"), Colossians 2:15 ("rulers"), and Jude 6 ("own domain")—as well as its apparent contrast with the term that precedes it here (angels)—seems to indicate fallen angels, the demons. If so, Paul is saying that no supernatural created being, good or evil, can sever our relationship to Christ.

Things present and **things to come** represent everything we are experiencing and will yet experience.

Powers translates *dunamis*, the ordinary Greek word for power. But in its plural form, as here, it often refers to miracles or mighty deeds. It was also used figuratively of persons in positions of authority and power. Regardless of the specific meaning Paul had in mind here, **powers** represents another obstacle that Christians need not fear.

Paul may have used **height** and **depth** as astrological terms that were familiar in his day, *hupsōma* (**height**) referring to the high point, or zenith, of a star's path, and *bathos* (**depth**) to its lowest point. If so, the idea is that Christ's love secures a believer from the beginning to the end of life's path. Or perhaps he used the terms to signify the infinity of space, which is endless in every direction. In either case, the basic meaning is that of totality.

To leave no doubt that security is all-encompassing, Paul adds **nor any other created thing.** Since only God Himself is uncreated, everyone else and everything else is excluded.

There is nothing anywhere at any time that **shall be able to separate us from the love of God, which is in Christ Jesus our Lord.** Our salvation was secured by God's decree from eternity past and will be held secure by Christ's love through all future time and throughout all eternity.

Earlier in this epistle Paul declared that, "as it is written, 'There is none righteous, not even one; there is none who understands, there is none who seeks for God; all have turned aside, together they have become useless; there is none who does good.'" To make sure that no person could make an exception for himself, the apostle added, "there is not even one" (Rom 3:10–12). In a similar way, Paul allows absolutely no exceptions in regard to the believer's security in Christ.

In this marvelous closing section of chapter 8, verses 31–34 focus on the love of God the Father, and verses 35–39 focus on the love of God the Son. One is reminded of Jesus' high priestly prayer, in which He prays on behalf of believers, "that they may all be one; even as Thou, Father, art in Me, and I in Thee, that they also may be in Us; ... And the glory which Thou hast given Me I have given to them; that they may be one, just as We are one; I in them, and Thou in Me, that they may be perfected in unity, that the world may know that Thou didst send Me, and didst love them, even as Thou didst love Me. Father, I desire that they also, whom Thou hast given Me, be with Me where I am" (John 17:21–24).

George Matheson was born in Glasgow, Scotland, in 1842. As a child he had only partial vision, and his sight became progressively worse, until it resulted in blindness by the time he was eighteen. Despite his handicap, he was a brilliant student and graduated from the University of Glasgow and later from seminary. He became pastor of several churches in Scotland, including a large church in Edinburgh, where he was greatly respected and loved. After he had been engaged to a young woman for a short while, she broke the engagement, having decided she could not be content married to a blind man. Some believe that this painful disappointment in romantic love led Matheson to write the beautiful hymn which begins with the following stanza:

> O love that will not let me go,
> I rest my weary soul in Thee;
> I give Thee back the life I owe,
> That in Thine ocean depths its flow
> May richer, fuller be.

Because our God is infinite in power and love, "we confidently say, 'The Lord is my helper, I will not be afraid. What shall man do to me?'" (Heb 13:6). Because our God is infinite in power and love, we can say with David, "When I am afraid, I will put my trust in Thee" (Ps 56:3) and, "In peace I will both lie down and sleep, for Thou alone, O Lord, dost make me to dwell in safety" (Ps 4:8). Because our God is infinite in power and love, we can say with Moses, "The eternal God is a dwelling place, and underneath are the everlasting arms" (Deut 33:27). Because our God is infinite in power and love, we can say with the writer of Hebrews, "This hope we have as an anchor of the soul, a hope both sure and steadfast" (Heb 6:19).

BIBLIOGRAPHY

Alleine, Joseph. *The Alarm to Unconverted Sinners.* 1672. Reprint, Grand Rapids: Baker, 1980.

Barnhouse, Donald Grey. *Romans: Expositions of Bible Doctrines.* 2 vols. Peabody, MA: Hendrickson, 2013.

Baxter, Richard. *The Reformed Pastor.* Carlisle, PA: Banner of Truth, 1974.

Bonhoeffer, Dietrich. *The Cost of Discipleship.* New York: Macmillan, 1959.

Bruce, F. F. *The Letter of Paul to the Romans.* Grand Rapids: Eerdmans, 1985.

Calvin, John. *Commentary on the Epistle of Paul the Apostle to the Romans.* Grand Rapids: Baker, 1979.

——. *The Epistles of Paul the Apostle to the Romans and to the Thessalonians.* Grand Rapids: Eerdmans, 1960.

Cranfield, C. E. B. *A Critical and Exegetical Commentary on the Epistle to the Romans.* Edinburgh: T & T Clark, 1975.

Dana, H. E., and Mantey, Julius R. *A Manual Grammar of the Greek New Testament*. New York: Macmillan, 1927.

Edwards, Jonathan. *The Works of Jonathan Edwards*. Vol. 7, *The Life of David Brainerd*. Edited by Norman Pettit. New Haven: Yale University Press, 1985.

———. *The Works of Jonathan Edwards*. 2 vols. 1834. Reprint, Carlisle, PA: Banner of Truth, 1974.

Haldane, Robert. *An Exposition of the Epistle to the Romans*. MacDill AFB, FL: MacDonald, 1958.

Henry, Matthew. *Matthew Henry's Commentary on the Whole Bible*. Vol 6. Old Tappan, N.J.: Revell, n.d.

Hodge, Charles. *Commentary on the Epistle to the Romans*. Grand Rapids: Eerdmans, 1983.

Johnson, Alan F. *The Freedom Letter*. Chicago: Moody, 1974.

Lewis, C. S. *The Problem of Pain*. New York: Macmillan, 1962.

Lloyd-Jones, D. Martyn. *Romans: An Exposition of Chapter Six*. Grand Rapids: Zondervan, 1972.

Moule, Handley. *The Epistle to the Romans*. 1861. Reprint, Minneapolis: Klock & Klock Christian, 1982.

Murray, John. *The Epistle to the Romans*. Grand Rapids: Eerdmans, 1965.

———. *Principles of Conduct*. Grand Rapids: Eerdmans, 1957.

——. *Redemption Accomplished and Applied*. Grand Rapids: Eerdmans, 1955.

Newton, John. *Out of the Depths: An Autobiography*. Grand Rapids: Kregel, 1990.

Needham, David C. *Birthright: Christian Do You Know Who You Are?* Portland, OR: Multnomah, 1979.

Owen, John. *Sin and Temptation*. Portland, OR: Multnomah, 1983.

Pink, Arthur. *The Doctrines of Election and Justification*. Grand Rapids: Baker, 1974.

Stott, John R. W. *Our Guilty Silence*. Grand Rapids: Eerdmans, 1969.

Tozer, A. W. *The Root of the Righteous*. Harrisburg, PA: Christian, 1955.

Watson, Thomas. *A Body of Divinity*. Carlisle, PA: Banner of Truth, 1983.

——. *A Divine Cordial*. Grand Rapids: Baker, 1981.

Wilson, Geoffrey B. *Romans: A Digest of Reformed Comment*. London: Banner of Truth, 1969.

Wuest, Kenneth S. *Romans in the Greek New Testament*. Grand Rapids: Eerdmans, 1955.

——. *Wuest's Word Studies from the Greek New Testament*. Vol. 1. Grand Rapids: Eerdmans, 1973.

INDEXES

INDEX OF SCRIPTURE

INDEXES

INDEX OF SUBJECTS

Adam,
before the Fall, 35
representative of human race, 4, 14–15, 94, 117, 193
Adoption, Roman, 84, 87, 96
Afflictions, of Christian, 103, 106, 109, 229
Angels, 96, 115, 158, 239–240
Apocalypse of Baruch, 114
Assurance of salvation, 64–65, 70, 72, 78–79, 81, 85–88, 107, 138, 211, 234
Atonement,
Day of, 16
substitutionary, 22, 211, 224

Baptism, baptized, 13–14, 181
Barnhouse, Donald Grey, 238
Baxter, Richard, 53
Behavior, Spirit-controlled, 42, 67–68
Belief, true, 74
Believer
battle with sin and Satan, 8
judgment of, 12, 17
work of Holy Spirit in, 26–27, 33–35
Bray, Billy, 88

Call, nature of God's, 180, 187, 202
Chantry, Walter J., 33
Christ
Adam, antithetical relationship with, 14–15
perfect priesthood of, 16, 100, 144, 225, 241
second coming, 100
Christian life
remaining humanness in, 20, 48, 62, 117, 122, 126, 131, 133, 140, 144
Christians
afflictions of, 103, 106–107, 109
conflict with the flesh, 35
confession of sins by, 64
divine discipline of, 11, 155, 165
false, 59, 230, 236
perseverance of, 233

spiritual responsibility of, 35, 54
Conscience, 74
Conviction of sin, 71–72, 74
Creator, God as, 39, 98, 118, 212

Damnation, predestination and, 193, 203
Day of Atonement, 16
Death
fear of, deliverance from, 80
spiritual, 19, 45, 56, 233
Decision for Christ, 195, 201
Deeper life, 61
Discipline
divine, 11, 155, 160, 165
Donne, John, 80
Doubt
believers', 138, 140

Earth, destiny of in God's hands, 119, 121
Edwards, Jonathan, 44
Entropy, evolution and, 120
Environmentalism, 118
Eternal security, 150–151, 171, 177, 206
Evolution, 120
Examination, self-, 57

Faith, true, 56, 172
Faithfulness, cost of, 160, 231
Fall of man, 2, 35, 94, 113, 117–118
Fear of death, deliverance from, 80
Flesh
Christian's battle with, 35
Christian's victory over, 233
Foreordination, 198–199
Forgiveness, 10, 58, 170, 172–173, 203, 219

Glorification
justification and, 93, 206
ultimate, 93–94, 130, 138–139, 156, 186, 189, 194, 207

the
MACARTHUR
NEW TESTAMENT
COMMENTARY

THE MACARTHUR NEW TESTAMENT COMMENTARY series
is a verse-by-verse exposition of the New Testament that brings
the believer into fellowship with God. Written for pastor
and layperson alike, every commentary examines the history,
language, and theology of the text to provide an accurate
interpretation of each passage. The goal is for the believer to
understand and apply God's Word to daily life in order to be
conformed to the image of the Lord Jesus Christ.

JOHN MACARTHUR PUBLISHING GROUP
LOS ANGELES, CALIFORNIA